AFFECTIVE EDUCATION:
METHODS
AND TECHNIQUES

AFFECTIVE EDUCATION:
METHODS
AND TECHNIQUES

Edited by

ISADORE L. SONNIER, B.A., M.Ed., Ed.D.
Professor of Science Education
University of Southern Mississippi
Hattiesburg, Mississippi 39406-8202

Educational Technology Publications
Englewood Cliffs, New Jersey 07632

Library of Congress Cataloging-in-Publication Data

Affective education: methods and techniques

  Bibliography: p.
  Includes index.
  1. Affective education. 2. Education—Aims and objec-
tives. 3. Holism. I. Sonnier, Isadore L.
LB1073.A34 1989   370.11   88-24407
ISBN 0-87778-212-1

Printed in the United States of America.

Library of Congress Catalog Card Number:
88-24407.

International Standard Book Number:
0-87778-212-1.

First Printing: January, 1989.

CONTRIBUTORS

Isadore L. Sonnier, B.A., M.Ed., Ed.D., Editor
   Department of Science Education
   University of Southern Mississippi

Isadore L. Sonnier earned the B.A. degree in Upper Elementary Education from the University of Southwestern Louisiana (USL) in 1955, the M.Ed. degree in Educational Administration and Educational Psychology from Louisiana State University in 1958, and the Ed.D. degree in Science Education/Earth Science from the University of Northern Colorado in 1966.

He has had a continuing interest in meeting the elusive needs of individual differences in education. Besides numerous publications on this topic for the past 15 years, he has published in two books: *Holistic Education: Teaching of Science in the Affective Domain,* Philosophical Library Press, 1982, and (Ed.) *Methods and Techniques of Holistic Education,* Charles C. Thomas, 1985. Sonnier also has ongoing interests in the atmospheric sciences and has published topics on lightning, alpen glow, and the jet streams.

Project Innovation has awarded him a citation in the *College Student Journal* (Spring, 1984) for his accomplishments as a science educator at USM. He was honored in 1986 as the outstanding alumnus of the College of Education at USL for the years 1954-56.

He is presently serving as Professor in the Department of Science Education, where he teaches science for non-science students and earth science education for teachers. He has served USM since 1967 and with National Science Foundation funding, was instrumental in teacher preparation throughout the state toward implementing earth science in the middle and junior high school curricula. He is director of The Consortium on the Study of Holistic Education.

Craig A. Buschner, B.S., M.S., Ed.D., Assistant Editor
    Department of Physical Education
    University of Southern Mississippi
    Hattiesburg, MS 39406-5034

Giovanni Fontecchio, B.S., M.A., Ph.D., Assistant Editor
    Department of Foreign Languages
    University of Southern Mississippi
    Hattiesburg, MS 39406-5038

Linda H. Kay, B.S., M.S., Ed.S., Ed.D., Assistant Editor
    English and Social Studies Teacher
    Forrest County Agricultural High School
    Brooklyn, MS 39425

Rex Leonard, B.S., M.S., Ph.D., Assistant Editor
    Department of Educational Leadership and Research
    University of Southern Mississippi
    Hattiesburg, MS 39406-5027

Saundra Y. McGuire, B.S., M.A., Ph.D., Assistant Editor
    Department of Chemistry
    Alabama A & M University
    Normal, AL 35762

Patty M. Ward, B.S., M.S., Ph.D. Candidate, Assistant Editor
    College of Education and Psychology
    University of Southern Mississippi
    Hattiesburg, MS 39406-7634

Lisardo Doval Salgado, B.S., M.A., Ph.D.,
    Instituto de Ciencias de la Educacion,
    Universidad de Santiago de Compostela,
    Avda. Juan XXIII, s/n,
    Santiago-La Coruna, SPAIN

Martha G. Dow, B.S., M.Ed., Ph.D.
Foreign Language Teacher
Petal High School
Petal, MS 39465

Elaine F. Fish, B.S., M.S., Ed.D. Candidate
Department of Science Education
University of Southern Mississippi
Science Teacher
Petal High School
Petal, MS 39465

Tressie S. Harper, A.A., B.S., M.Ed.
English Teacher
Lilly Burney Magnet School
Hattiesburg, MS 39401

Jean A. Haspeslagh, B.S.N., M.S.Ed., M.S., D.N.S. Candidate
Louisiana State University, Medical Center
School of Nursing, New Orleans, LA
University of Southern Mississippi
School of Nursing
Hattiesburg, MS 39406-5095

Frank F. Montalvo, B.A., M.S.W., D.S.W.
Director of Intercultural Institute for Training and Research
Worden School of Social Service
Our Lady of the Lake University
San Antonio, TX 78285

Miguel A. Santos Rego, M.A., Ph.D.,
Dept. de Pedegogia Sistematica,
Instituto de Ciencias de la Educacion,
Universidad de Santiago de Compostela,
Avda. Juan XXIII, s/n,
Santiago-La Coruna, SPAIN.

Renato A. Schibeci, B.S., M.Sc., M.Ed., Ph.D.
    School of Education
    Murdoch University
    Murdoch, WESTERN AUSTRALIA 6150

Douglas W. Schipull, B.S., M.A., Ed.S., Ph.D. Candidate
    Department of Curriculum and Instruction, U.S.M.
    Learning Disability Teacher
    Pensacola High School
    Pensacola, FL 32506

Luis Sobrado Fernandez, B.S., M.A., Ph.D.,
    Director de el Instituto de Ciencias de la Educacion,
    Universidad de Santiago de Compostela,
    Galicia, SPAIN.

Claudine B. Sonnier, B.S., M.S., Ed.S.
    Home Economics Teacher
    Forrest County Agricultural High School
    Brooklyn, MS 39425

David L. Sonnier, B.S.
    JFK Special Warfare Center
    Fort Bragg
    Fayetteville, NC 20307

David R. Stronck, B.S., M.S., Ph.D.
    Department of Teacher Education
    California State University-Hayward
    Hayward, CA 94542

Gary D. Taber, A.B., M.Ed.
    Coordinator of Foreign Languages
    Anne Arundel County Schools
    2644 River Road
    Annapolis, MD 21401

Dorothy M. Wesselmann, B.A., M.S.
    Science Teacher
    E. T. Booth Middle School
    Woodstock, GA 30188

Martha A. Wittenauer, B.S.N., M.S.N., Ed.D.
    Associate Dean of Graduate Programs
    College of Nursing
    University of Arkansas for Medical Sciences
    4301 West Markham Street
    Little Rock, AR 72205

PREFACE

Student achievement is almost always expressed in terms of how much was learned—the quantity. Rarely is student achievement expressed in affective terms—the quality of that learning. Students emerge from any learning situation in one of three affective states; they perceive either positive, neutral, or negative feelings *about themselves with relation to the subject matter presented.* An understanding of the factors that lead students to these perceived states could diminish the widespread confusion about affective education. Such an understanding would also shed light on how to implement, administer and maintain positive affective results.

The state of affective perception can be observed to differ for each learner within a particular group, even if the learners experience common exposure to content and mode of presentation. It is known that each student differs with respect to learning ability, personal motivation and satisfaction, as well as to the response elicited from the manner and mode of presentation.

Sadly, though unintentionally, subject matter is often presented so as to elicit negative affective results. For example, the teacher may feel obligated to maintain "high subject matter standards" or the need to keep up with a syllabus prepared without the benefit of knowing the ability of the students to be taught. The teacher, then, faced with cutting mastery time short or "just covering" the material, sacrifices the former and achieves the latter. The unanticipated by-product, of course, is a room full of frustrated students who show their frustration by hating the class, the teacher, the materials studied, and everything and everyone connected with the experience.

To this, I share the observation that any human being who does *physical* or *psychological* harm to another is considered a felon — the injustice, a felony. Can we be no less concerned with teaching efforts that evoke negative affective results? All educators must become aware that subject matter presented at a time and in a way beyond the students' abilities to grasp, can cause the pain of frustration and elicit negative affective results.

Schooling can be a psychologically devastating place for many at the primary level. By middle and junior high school, students are institutionalized with psychological violation as a norm. We share with educators at all levels that few, if any, students are too immature to learn materials appropriate to their level and that any failure in learning on the part of a student is really a failure to teach on the part of the teacher.

Although highly analytical students have the kind of thought processing that normally succeeds in school, too many of them emerge from the system with problems that are caused by the widespread misunderstanding of affective education. This insensitivity to negative affective results has far reaching and even devastating effects on the lives of too many individuals at all levels of education.

The students' affects can no longer be ignored. Attention to its implementation would, in my estimation, ease some of the heavy burden borne by today's classroom teachers. To bring joy and pleasure to the learning process (the positive affect) can never be too much to ask of a teacher. Neutral affective results are minimum expectation. To elicit or inflict negative results in students is unacceptable and may reflect a teacher's need for supervisory assistance.

This project on affective education is an outgrowth of two previous projects: *Holistic Education: Teaching of Science in the Affective Domain* (Sonnier, 1982b) and *Methods and Techniques of Holistic Education* (Sonnier, 1985a). Holistic education is a by-product of the scientific breakthroughs of the mid-1950's concerning human hemisphericity and lateral dominance in thinking and learning. However, as in medicine, scientific breakthroughs are not instantly applicable breakthroughs. Consequently, much research, discussion, and clarification are needed before these findings can eventually gain utility at the practical level.

The hemispheric nature of humans explains WHY holistic education simultaneously and concurrently stimulates the propensities of both hemispheres. This knowledge demands of all educators the implementation of holistic strategies so as to assist visual learners to become more analytical and analytical learners to become more visual and thus, the fulfillment of each's potential toward becoming well rounded and better adjusted individuals. Although this application of holistic educational strategies explains the HOW's with good reasoning, much more effort will be needed to bring about any degree of comprehensive implementation (see Chapter 17 for "HOW" to implement an affective program and see Chapter 18 for a definitive study on holistic education with affective results).

Because holistic educational strategies so easily promote and sustain AFFECTIVE RESULTS, the literature was searched for contributions in the areas of AFFECTIVE TEACHING AND LEARNING. Eighteen articles were uncovered in that search and the authors were solicited to contribute similar articles on the topic. This book is the result of those and other contributions, each written to fill a specific need in our total message.

Expressing for all of the contributors, I make the reader aware that AFFECTIVE EDUCATION is neither thoroughly nor completely covered by our efforts. However, our hope is that we have made at least a ripple on these still and latent waters of the educational enterprise.

I.L.S.

INTRODUCTION

While making logical determinations from the data on human cerebral hemisphericity, several conclusions emerge that pertain to teaching and learning. The conclusion that underlies all the others is that some people process their thoughts visually while others process theirs analytically. Visual thought processing appears to be the seat of creativity (visualizing the whole phenomenon and drawing conclusions from these mental images), while analytical thought processing appears to be the seat of constructive, linear-logical thinking. Evidence points to this being the basic structure for other traits of mutually exclusive dichotomies. An individual's basic approach toward learning, teaching, social behavior, and leadership, then, is basically dependent on whether his/her hemispherical preference is visual or analytical. Further, the more of any one of these dichotomous traits one has, the less is the potential for the other.

All superior-subordinate transactions, such as boss/secretary, employer/employee, principal/teacher, teacher/student, are heavily dependent on the former's understanding of his/her own hemispherical preference and those of the subordinate for successful interaction. Our concern here focuses on educational settings because many students at all educational levels from pre-school to post-graduate studies have suffered psychological brutalization, hurt, and frustration simply because their hemispheric preference for learning differed from their teacher's hemispheric preference for teaching. It is our view that this condition must not continue. There is, for example, an institutionalized tendency in primary school to think of

visually oriented first graders as appearing more immature than their analytically oriented counterpart. The stigma created at this level is generally
reinforced in higher grades until the student is convinced that the limitations in his/her achievement are due to the basic lack of intelligence rather
than a hemispherical preference different from the teachers'. The tragedy
occurs as a result of teachers' lack of understanding of holistic education
which advocates strategies that can prevent, or at least solve many educational problems that result from differences in hemispherical preference. Holistic education, the teaching of both cerebral hemispheres simultaneously and
concurrently, has the further benefit of promoting positive affective results.

Tradition has it that there should be as many A's as F's, B's as D's, and
C's indicate average achievement. We propose a different model: *The teacher
is paid to teach 100% of the students and it is our estimation that well over 80%
cognitive achievement/affective attainment in 80% of the time would all but
eliminate considering the school as a hurting place–a place for failure and the in-
fliction of other psychological harm. If a student is allowed his/her perspective of
personal and attentive applications at the time of learning, this level of learning,
referred to as metacognitive development,* is within reach.

We discuss holistic education and metacognitive development as neuroeducation. It is our desire to share these far reaching implications of neuroeducation because it is on the forefront of contemporary education. Individual
differences and different individuals need no longer be the puzzle or the
maze of past consideration. We are committed to the ideal that the dispen-
sation of high quality education is for everyone.

I.L.S.

ACKNOWLEDGEMENTS

I wish to thank the many contributors to our project. Without their kind cooperation, patience and gracious assistance, this project could not have been completed. During the course of the two years in preparation, the many persons who have been helpful make it difficult to single out each and every one of them. The assistance of Ann T. Georgian, Assistant Principal at Hawkins Junior High School, Hattiesburg, MS, and two teachers, Tressie Harper and Lorraine Rigsby is appreciated.

I also wish to acknowledge the assistance of Velma J. Lashbrook of the Wilson Learning Corporation, with deep appreciation.

Gratitude is expressed to those who helped in the editorial process of our book: Craig Buschner, Giovanni Fontecchio, Rex Leonard, Saundra McGuire, and especially to Patty Ward and Linda Kay.

Special thanks to Martha Dow, Giovanni Fontecchio, Emilio Ramos and Esteban Patino Perez who spent tedious hours translating English to Spanish and Spanish to English while keeping the important link alive and fruitful with colleagues in Spain.

Special thanks also to Henry Goodwin for personal and professional attention to the lithographic preparation of this manuscript and to Linda Kay for its final editorial supervision.

And to my dearest and lifelong friend, my wife, Claudine, for always being at my side — a master teacher whose treasured critique of my work is not always heeded, but always appreciated — I express my deepest admiration and appreciation.

I.L.S.

CONTENTS

LIST OF FIGURES AND TABLES

AFFECTIVE EDUCATION: METHODS AND TECHNIQUES

AFFECTIVE EDUCATION: METHODS AND TECHNIQUES

Isadore L. Sonnier, Editor

PART I

INTRODUCTION AND OVERVIEW OF INSTRUCTIONAL DESIGN AND OUTCOMES

Giovanni Fontecchio, Editor

All activities of the educational enterprise have been widely accepted as pertaining to one or more of the three domains: the cognitive, the affective, or the psychomotor. This taxonomy has served education well. Instructional management has evolved almost exclusively as a tool of cognitive achievement. However, with the advent and understanding of individual differences due to hemisphericity, we have available insight into the management of both, cognitive achievement and the attainment of positive affective results (Chapter 1). Evidence is pointing to the probability that individual differences in such areas as thinking, learning, social styles, and even teaching modes are functions of hemispheric preference (Chapter 2). Holistic educational strategies have the unique potential to meet these individual differences needs for both the teacher and the learner (Chapter 3).

G. F.

THE EDUCATIONAL TAXONOMIES

Jean A. Haspeslagh and Martha A. Wittenauer

The need to classify the learning process stems from educators having a natural desire to know more precisely the results of their teaching efforts. In the mid-1950's, educators started to satisfy this need by categorizing certain cognitive activities in a scalar methodology to understand more completely the building process at each level in the activities of learning. Through the work of Bloom, Krathwohl, Masia, and others, a project was culminated in 1956 with the publication of the first of two handbooks categorizing educational objectives. *Handbook I* was created as a taxonomy of objectives in the cognitive domain and was instantly an enormous step forward in assisting with educational management.

In time, "Bloom's *Taxonomy*," as it came to be called, became better understood as honest efforts were made by educators at all levels to gain the desperately desired firm grip on educational objectives. One of the obvious contributions, among many, was that more and more educators began to question traditional strategies and outcomes, coupled with an even closer eye on content delivery. A firmer grip on these aspects of teaching was evolved into a preoccupation with the cognitive achievement of students, for which results which could be easily tested.

Handbook I: The Cognitive Domain. In the first book, six levels in the cognitive domain of learning are described. These levels facilitated the development of teaching goals and objectives, while at the same time provided some structure whereby there may be an achievement of balance in any learning program (Litwack, Linc & Bower, 1985).

Bloom's *Taxonomy* also served as a catalyst in the search for a better way to evaluate teaching and learning. For example, Dressel (1976) described the cognitive domain in two major categories. The first category, knowledge, expanding on Bloom's first level, was further delineated into thirteen types of knowledge. Bloom's five other levels, comprehension, application, analysis, synthesis and evaluation, were consolidated into the second major category, intellectual abilities and skills. The order of these levels is based on the complexity of the task involved. In most cases, some proficiency in the previous level is required before one can use or understand the next level.

We provide an example of Bloom's (1956) taxonomy of the cognitive domain. In these specific categories, one can relate each cognitive activity to a specific conceptual framework. For example, in the process of decision making, one can identify apparent differences in levels of cognitive activity (see Figure 1.1 for levels, definitions and examples).

The writers of Bloom's *Taxonomy* could not have taken hemispheric preference into consideration simply because it was not yet discovered. And, one would think that the concept of hemisphericity is not applicable, especially since there appears to be a very constructive and analytical approach to the development of the various levels of learning. However, both the visual and analytical processes of the hemispheres are indeed utilized at every level in the learning process. Therefore, it behooves us, as teachers, to assist our students toward this holistic development of the learning process at every level. Further, the structuring of learning objectives, with this added attention to the level of visual and analytical understanding, called holistic strategies, may contribute significantly to the students' cognitive achievements (see Chapter 2 for this rationale).

Handbook II: The Affective Domain. The second handbook was a taxonomy of objectives in the affective domain, published in 1964 (Krathwohl, et al.). While helpful, these efforts created but a fraction of the impact as compared to the first handbook on the cognitive domain. Due to the difficulty in quantifying a student's progress in the affective domain, teachers have often avoided and even resisted attempts to try to establish educational objectives dealing with this domain. The difficulty of obtaining hard data on

THE COGNITIVE DOMAIN

Level	Definition	Example
1. KNOWLEDGE	Recall of specifics and universals, recall of methods and processes, or the recall of a pattern, structures and setting.	Identification of the components of the decision-making process.
2. COMPREHENSION	Knowledge of that being communicated and can make use of material without necessarily relating it to other materials.	Description of each component of the decision-making process.
3. APPLICATION	In use of the concept in particular and concrete situations. This may be in the form of general ideas, rules of procedures or general methods.	Use of the decision-making process in an activity.
4. ANALYSIS	The breakdown of a concept into its constituent parts such that the relative hierarchy of ideas is made clear and the relations between ideas expressed are made explicit.	See each segment of the decision-making process as it relates to the whole and identify its relationship to each segment.
5. SYNTHESIS	The putting together of elements and parts so as to form a whole.	Integration of process of decision-making with review of actual out- comes of activity as a whole.
6. EVALUATION	Judgements about the value and methods for given purposes.	Compare actual results with anticipated results of decision-making process and identify variances.

FIGURE 1.1

the learner's emotions and feelings became largely an admission that "it can't be done." But most often, "the lack of its importance" was relegated to "I don't have time." For many reasons, the students' affects remain unchartered territory.

The effects of this benign neglect of the affective domain have resulted in a tendency for educational efforts to be focused on the more readily assessable cognitive domain. *Handbook II* was devoted to the affective domain. As with the cognitive domain, they described five levels: receiving, responding, valuing, organization, and characterization by a value or value complex (see Figure 1.2, page 10).

THE AFFECTIVE DOMAIN

Level	Definition	Example
1. RECEIVING	Sensitivity to and a willingness to take in or attend to certain phenomena.	Is attentive when others speak. Demonstrates awareness of aesthetics. Alert to human values.
2. RESPONDING	Reacting to a phenomenon with an overt response.	Shows signs of enjoying music, art, etc. Accepts responsibility for own learning.
3. VALUING	Consistently attaches worth to (belief in) a phenomenon.	Agrees education is of value and volunteers to attend optional classes for own benefit.
4. ORGANIZATION	Beginning of the development of an organized value system.	Able to weigh alternative and develop plan to meet specific needs.
5. CHARACTERIZATION BY A VALUE OR VALUE COMPLEX	Synthesis and internalization of a value system.	Able to judge issues in the context in which they occur. Develop own philosophy.

FIGURE 1.2

In dealing with the affective domain, one soon finds that these are the same areas that are dominant in individuals who are visual perceivers. It would therefore appear to be imperative that educators retain an interest in the affective domain as well as the cognitive domain in order to avoid disenfranchising an important segment of the student population. How can educators, who are themselves either visually or analytically oriented, begin to meet the needs of two such diverse groups of learners? The first step is to recognize that these differences do exist. Second, it is important to recognize that the individual who is analytically oriented may tend to relate more readily to the linear-logical, analytical aspects of the cognitive domain. Visually oriented individuals may tend to relate more readily to graphic descriptions and may as well be more sensitive to affective qualities. Third, and of great importance, one must realize that neither orientation is right nor wrong, better or worse. Both exist and need to be attended to in the teaching-learning process. Awareness of the educational taxonomies can assist the educator by serving as a reminder of the usefulness of the cognitive and affective domains as aids in the development of educational objectives.

They serve only as *aids* in the evaluation of teacher-made objectives and the students' accomplishments of these objectives. They are not to be used as the means for measuring students' learning outcomes. Bloom's *Taxonomy* has certainly served educators with a great deal of clarity and conciseness in coupling objectives with educational outcomes. However, this understanding rests almost, if not entirely, on content delivery on the part of the teacher and cognitive achievement on the part of the student. The fact remains that this noble advancement does not take into consideration individual differences among students, much less the level of affective attainment.

Measuring Cognitive Results in Affective Terms. Sonnier, Fontecchio and Dow explain that one basic difference among learners is the fact that some are visually oriented and others are analytically oriented. This fact was neither considered traditionally, nor in the application of teaching objectives toward cognitive achievement, or any other outcome. They propose the consideration that there are only four levels of learning outcomes (see Chapter 17). The students:

1. Learned a lot and enjoyed the learning experience.
2. Learned a lot, but did not enjoy the experience.
3. Learned little, but enjoyed the experience.
4. Learned little and did not enjoy the experience.

Further, it is proposed that educational outcomes need not be shrouded in complex levels of affective attainment. There are but three and they are easily understood by any classroom teacher. Affective results are always in one of three attainment levels: positive, neutral, or negative. These outcomes are easily measured for both, collectively for a group of learners, or for individual learners. The students complete a learning experience with one of the following feelings:

1. Positive about themselves and the experience.
2. Neutral, or
3. Negative about themselves and the experience.

An instrument was developed to obtain these data from students (see Chapter 17 for further discussion of the instruments used to make these determinations). From these data, any classroom teacher of students at any level beyond the reading age, can quickly assess the students for these results and know exactly the affective level of attainment. For pre-readers, the simple question, "Did you enjoy learning this lesson?", will be sufficient.

The regular weekly or progress testing, coupled with an affective attainment inquiry, instantly gives a teacher at any level the results of that teaching effort and indeed a possibility to grow in deficient areas. This kind of personal supervision should be done on a regular basis at all levels. However, it is our experience that few teachers can reach 100% of the students 100% of the time. The present understanding of these instruments in educational management is that 80% achievement 80% of the time is very good. The conclusion that can be drawn is that, by taking advantage of students' feedback on affective behavior, positive educational outcomes are at the grasp of any teacher who honestly wishes to teach all students. It is suggested that both visual and analytical students can be reached through holistic educational strategies (see Chapter 3) and that educational outcomes are easily quantified through the assessment of students' achievement, real and/or perceived, coupled with their reported level of affective attainments. Furthermore, any teacher at any level of service can use and find potential for growth in this process.

CHAPTER 2

HEMISPHERICITY: A KEY TO UNDERSTANDING INDIVIDUAL DIFFERENCES AMONG TEACHERS & LEARNERS

Isadore L. Sonnier

In its brief history, human cerebral hemisphericity has attracted much attention in all of the social sciences, including education. Numerous contributors have amassed a rather large volume of literature and have created a notable amount of controversy (Gazzaniga, 1975; Keefe, 1982; Sonnier, 1982a, 1982b, 1984, 1985a). Educators are searching not only to further identify more of these hemispheric specializations, but, more importantly, educators are seeking ways to apply this knowledge in their own teaching and learning activities. Hemispheric dominance may well be one of the most important factors to consider toward a better understanding of individual differences among ourselves as teachers and our students.

A review of selected literature is presented as I share some personal applications of hemisphericity and point to hemisphericity as the basis for holistic education—the teaching of the whole person. Holistic education goes beyond the incorporation of the term "confluent education." It identifies the loci of that embodiment in which both affective and cognitive aspects are integrated and flow together (see Romey, 1976). Further, in that context, holistic education becomes synonymous with the expression "humanistic education" (see Hassard, 1985).

Hemisphericity is the term implying "the intriguing possibility that individuals have a tendency to appeal to one hemisphere and its mode of thought more than the other," according to Krashen (1977, p. 121), a "term (which he) borrowed from Bogen, DeZure, TenHouten, and March (1972)." Since then, significant misunderstandings have obstructed the utility and applicabililty of hemisphericity in education.

The first among these obstacles was quick to surface. The left hemisphere was immediately dubbed the *major hemisphere* and the right hemisphere was relegated to the *subordinate, minor hemisphere*. While there is yet the hint of this lingering misunderstanding, the propensities of both hemispheres are today widely accepted as parallel, equal, and orchestrated entities. The second obstacle is a perpetuated misconception by an educational system which ignores or excludes the right hemispheric functions and processes. In Nebes' (1975) words, "perhaps we are short-changing ourselves when we educate only left-sided talents in basic schooling. . . the inverse relationship between scholastic achievement and creativity. . . overtraining for verbal skills at the expense of nonverbal abilities" (p. 16).

The Nature of Human Brain Hemispheres. The natural division of the brain into the right and left hemispheres has long been a cause for speculation among researchers in behavior and learning. The resulting dichotomy "has a sound physiologic basis. . . (with) two principal and different types of cognition, each typically identifiable with one of the two cerebral hemispheres" (Bogen, 1977, p. 137). Each is the seat of complex sets of operations, orchestrating the thought processes and body functions. The *split-brain* research, as it has come to be called, was initiated in 1960 when Dr. Joseph Bogen proposed that the brain be split (the corpus callosum sectioned) "for the purpose of controlling the interhemispheric spread of epilepsy" (Gazzaniga, 1975, p. 10).

Subsequent psychological testing of these patients revealed hemispheric dichotomies which Nebes (1975) described as "symbolic versus visual-spatial, associative versus apperceptive, propositional versus appositional, and analytic versus gestalt (suggesting). . . that the organization and processing of data by the right hemisphere is in predisposition for perceiving the total rather than the part. By contrast, the left hemisphere is seen to analyze input sequentially, abstracting out the relevant details and associating these with verbal symbols" (p. 15). Adding to the common knowledge that non-readers are predominantly visually oriented persons, Witelson (1977) reported evidence that children with developmental dyslexia were with two visual hemispheres rather than one of each. This gave rise to the potential possibility for highly analytical individuals to have two analytical hemispheres rather than one of each. A normal curve population was assumed to exist with eclectic orchestration of these two extremes in the rest of the population. And, thus, one looks at the extremes for an understanding of the blended behaviors (Sonnier, 1982a, 1982b, 1984, 1985a).

Hemispheric Dichotomies in Educational Thought and Practice. Probably the most convincing evidence pointing to the relationships between the hemispheric phenomenon and the dichotomies in educational thought and practice arose from a compilation by Bogen (1975) in which he summarized the works of forty prominent authors "who have postulated two parallel 'ways of knowing' or two 'types of intelligence' or two 'cognitive styles'" (p. 25) (see Figure 2.1).

Sperry (awarded the Nobel Prize for his work in this area):

> The main theme to emerge . . . is that there appears to be two modes of thinking, verbal and non-verbal, represented rather separately in left and right hemispheres, respectively, and that our educational system, as well as science in general, tend to neglect the non-verbal form of intellect. What it comes down to is that modern society discriminates against the right hemisphere (p. 29).

While much of the foregoing discussion was taken from the important publication, *UCLA Educator* (Vol. 17, no. 2, 1975), yet another important publication appeared in 1982: *Student Learning Styles and Brain Behavior* (Keefe, 1982). Briefly, the programs, instrumentation and research of *learning styles* and *brain research* were updated and shared by representatives of the researchers and practitioners in these areas. However, applications of brain research were seldom mentioned as characteristic of or related to learning styles.

In one exception, Zenhausern (1982) reported that "neuroeducation is a term that can be applied to that aspect of education that focuses on the interaction of the brain and behavior in learning systems" (p. 192). For this contribution, he developed a questionnaire (patterned after Torrence et al.,

TERMS EMERGING IN THE LITERATURE DESCRIBING THE BEHAVIORAL FUNCTIONS OF THE TWO HEMISPHERES

Akhilinanda	buddi	manas
Assagioli	intellect	intuition
Austin	convergent	divergent
Bateson & Jackson	digital	analogic
Blackburn	intellectual	sensuous
Bronowski	deductive	imaginative
Bruner	rational	metaphoric
Cohen	analytic	rational
De Bono	vertical	horizontal
Deikman	active	receptive
Dieudonne	discrete	continuous
Freud	secondary	primary
Goldstein	abstract	concrete
Guilford	convergent	divergent
Hilgard	realistic	impulsive
Hobbes (per Murphy)	directed	free
Humphrey & Zangwill	propositional	imaginative
W. James	differential	existential
A. Jensen	transformational	associative
Kagan & Moss	analytic	rational
D. Lee	lineal	nonlineal
Levi-Strauss	positive	mythic
Levy & Sperry	analytic	gestalt
Lomas & Berkowitz	differentiation	integration
McFie, Piercy (from Spearman)	relations	correlates
McKellar	realistic	autistic
Maslow	rational	intuitive
Neisser	sequential	multiple
Oppenheimer	historical	timeless
Ornstein	analytic	holistic
Pavlov	second signaling	first signaling
C.S. Peirce	explicative	ampliative
Polanyi	explicit	tacit
Price	reductionist	compositionist
Radhakrishnan (per H.Smith)	rational	integral
Reusch	discursive	eidetic
Schenov (per Luria)	successive	simultaneous
Schopenhauer	objective	subjective
C.S. Smith	atomistic	gross
Wells	hierarchical	heterarchical

FIGURE 2.1

1977) which discerns *hemispheric preference*. Neuroeducation is herein designated as holistic education with metacognitive development, the students' awareness of knowledge acquisition (Ausubel, 1968; Di Vesta and Finke, 1985). In educational management, it is hemisphericity based instructional management with accountability.

Dunn, et al., (1977) had earlier discussed hemispheric preference as the newest element of *learning styles* and predicted that, as teachers begin to respond to the knowledge and understanding of what differences in hemispheric preference reveal about students, its importance "is likely to gain increasing attention among those who are concerned about providing maximum instructional opportunities for all" (p. 293).

On Implementing the Hemisphericity Model. Among the early implementors of the hemisphericity model in education, Spirduso (1978) should be recognized for the scholarly treatment of hemispheric lateralization in compensatory and voluntary movement—a consideration of the psychomotor domain. Edward's (1979) insight in art education was significant, as judged by the substantial popular influence that she generated. Vitale (1982) implemented a thorough understanding and treatment of hemisphericity in early childhood and lower elementary education. She provided many tests for learning styles and a broad and general implementation of the hemisphericity model at these early ages. Williams (1983) should also be mentioned for some practical interpretations of hemisphericity research as it applies to teaching and learning.

However, in reviewing Vitale and Williams, it became apparent that throughout the literature, it is widely accepted that visual persons learn *visually* and that analytical persons learn *auditorily*. The assumption is that those who make better grades are better listeners. The reference is to the senses, visual and auditory, and is misleading. Reference should be made to hemispheric preference and the mode of thinking and learning, *visual and analytical*. Drawing from observation and experience, it is safe to say that properly motivated, visual learners can become acutely auditory. In addition to their having keen visual adaptation, these students can become voracious learners.

This may explain why it is difficult to discriminate student achievement as a means of hemispheric determination. These data are most often rather bland in that not all analyticals are good students, nor are all visuals poor students. For these reasons, I point to *the processes of the hemispheres, rather than to the sensory organs as the loci of learning experiences and thus the seat of learning styles.* Therefore, one should speak of *"visual and analytical learners,"* in verification of hemisphericity as the basis for thinking and learning styles, as well as social styles and teaching modes, and perhaps other traits yet to be identified.

Aside from any discussion of "nurture," or environmental factors that contribute to personality development and individual differences, hemisphericity is in all probability the "nature" key to understanding individual differences among students and their teachers, too. However, the literature may be flawed with misconceptions that prevent progress in its implementation and application. Further, it is my experience that one must examine the two extremes of hemispheric preference/dominance, highly visual and highly analytical, in order to understand the blended middle of what appears to be a normal curve distribution. It is also my experience that these are the only persons that are *very sure* of their thought processing mode. Those with an eclectic blend, and with one or the other dominant, are *reasonably sure* of their dominance. However, those individual with an apparently equal blend are not only not sure, they are simply unable to explain their thinking mode. However, when made aware of the two systems, they readily admit the orchestrated use of both modes of thought processing (see Chapter 15).

CHAPTER 3

HOLISTIC EDUCATION → AFFECTIVE RESULTS = TEACHING THE WHOLE PERSON

Isadore L. Sonnier and Giovanni Fontecchio

Different Students Need Different Formats (Strategies) of Instruction

Establishing A Dichotomy of Differences Among Teachers. While conducting National Science Foundation earth science teacher preparation programs throughout the state of Mississippi, and prior to my knowledge of hemisphericity, in the late 1960s to early 1970s, I solicited self-reported data from many groups of teachers to determine some of the individual differences among teachers. Through these investigations, it was determined that between 35 to 40 percent of the teachers in each group felt satisfied and comfortable with being characterized as *Constructive* because of their step-by-step, methodical approach and life style. Once this group was established, and always in this order, approximately the same number from the remaining group was satisfied and comfortable to be characterized as *creative*, characteristically the absence of step-by-step, methodical approach and less structured lifestyle. Further, one of the distinguishing characteristics of this paradigm was that *constructive teachers* preferred to maintain an *authoritarian* (teacher-centered) *classroom atmosphere* and that *creative teachers* preferred to maintain a *self-directed* (student-centered) *atmosphere* in their classrooms (Sonnier, 1975, 1976).

A dichotomy of differences among students. In an attempt to relate thinking and learning styles with hemisphericity, a seven item test was developed
and designed to determine thinking and learning styles as being either visually
oriented or analytically oriented (Figure 3.1, see Leonard and Boulter, 1985).[1]
An update of these findings correlated with the hemisphericity model indicates that *constructivity* is an analytical person's thought processing mode
and that *creativity* is a visual person's thought processing mode (Sonnier,
1985a). It is now apparent that the two hemispheric propensities must be
examined in the relatively pure forms as found in highly visual and highly
analytical persons in order to be understood, rather than in the hybrid and
blended forms found in the remaining population at large.

Social styles (Lashbrook & Lashbrook, 1980) serve as another parameter
in need of further investigation to verify the structures of hemispheric preference. It appears that highly analytical persons display analytical social traits,
slightly analytical persons display the amiable social traits, slightly visual
persons display driver traits, and highly visual persons display expressive
traits. As presently understood, there are but a few individuals who display
these highly visual and highly analytical traits, as described by Leonard,
Ward and Schipull (see Chapter 15).

In self-reported and group interactions of college student groups conducted
since the late 1970s, there is emerging evidence that one's hemispheric preference also determines thinking, learning (Leonard and Boulter, 1985), social

---

[1] *Administering the Mode of Consciousness Test. Although this test for hemispheric preference com-
pares well with tests of similar intent by Torrence and Zenbausern (Leonard and Boulter, 1985),
there is yet much to be desired in getting good results. For example, best results are obtained if it
is administered several times. This is because of human nature, itself. Extremely visual and extremely analytical individuals have no difficulty in reporting their own hemispheric preferences.
However, these are relatively small populations. For all of the others in between, it is recommended
that the results of the first administration be discussed and then they be allowed time to make these
observations about themselves. An assumption that can be made is that, prior to this time, they
may have had no occasion to make such a consideration about themselves and, therefore, have no
such awareness. With some evidence, a further assumption has been that those individuals who have
and use both propensities the most, know and understand these processes the least. That is the basis
for our recommendation that the test be administered, the results discussed, and readministered at
two-week intervals for at least three times. Time in consideration appears to be an important factor
in the improvement of these self-reported data. This ongoing investigation is discussed in Chapter 15.*

MODE OF CONSCIOUSNESS

MOST PEOPLE USE ONE OF TWO BASIC WAYS OF THINKING, OR A
COMBINATION OF THE TWO. ON A SCALE OF 1 THROUGH 7,
SELECT THE EXPRESSION THAT BEST FITS YOUR OWN WAY OF THINKING

1 # VERY ANALYTICAL, LINEAR-LOGICAL, RATIONAL
(You line up your thoughts and reason them out)

7 # VERY VISUAL, HOLISTIC, INTUITIVE, CONFIGURATIONAL
(You can see the bits and pieces fall into the big picture)

4 # EQUAL USE OF BOTH WAYS

1. ANALYTICAL						VISUAL
(check 1	2	3	4	5	6	7
one) ( )	( )	( )	( )	( )	( )	( )

2. LOGICAL						HOLISTIC
(check 1	2	3	4	5	6	7
one) ( )	( )	( )	( )	( )	( )	( )

3. RATIONAL						INTUITIVE
(check 1	2	3	4	5	6	7
one) ( )	( )	( )	( )	( )	( )	( )

4. LINEAR-LOGICAL						CONFIGURATIONAL
(check 1	2	3	4	5	6	7
one) ( )	( )	( )	( )	( )	( )	( )

5. CONSTRUCTIVE						CREATIVE
(check 1	2	3	4	5	6	7
one) ( )	( )	( )	( )	( )	( )	( )

6. YOUR THINKING MODE FOR AS LONG AS YOU CAN REMEMBER:

ANALYTICAL/LOGICAL/RATIONAL				INTUITIVE/HOLISTIC/VISUAL		
(check 1	2	3	4	5	6	7
one) ( )	( )	( )	( )	( )	( )	( )

7. THE DEGREE THAT SCHOOLING HAS CHANGED YOUR WAY OF THINKING:

ANALYTICAL/LOGICAL/RATIONAL				INTUITIVE/HOLISTIC/VISUAL		
(check 1	2	3	4	5	6	7
one) ( )	( )	( )	( )	( )	( )	( )

FIGURE 3.1

styles (Chapter 29), and teaching styles. It appears that the constructivi-
ty/creativity paradigm of the earlier investigations (Sonnier, 1975, 1976)

can be further refined as an indication in hemispheric preference, providing some rationale as to why analytical teachers prefer teacher-centered strategies and visual teachers prefer student-centered strategies.

This also helps to explain why there is a relatively large, hybrid group in the middle of this normally distributed population. This is the blended mixture with eclectic tendencies who borrow from the two extreme, or pure forms of hemispheric preference. Most of these identify either as eclectic with authoritarian tendencies, or eclectic with self-directed tendencies (Sonnier, 1975; Leonard and Boulter, 1985).

Holistic Education: Meeting the Needs of All Students. The attributes of hemisphericity appear to be a major contributor to the determinations of individual differences among students and teachers alike. While there are two different preferred modes of teaching as expressed by these different individuals, there is a single set of teaching strategies that all can use toward reaching and teaching more students. Holistic educational strategies meet the instructional needs of all students, visual and analytical. These strategies meet the universal needs of students because of the extensive use of visual aids which meet the learning style needs of visual students. Also, there is simultaneously the presentation of a linear logical approach by thoroughly explaining each visual aid, thereby meeting the learning style needs of analytical students (Sonnier, 1982b, 1985a). Both teachers have the potential for frustrating students. The visual teacher may "jump around" pointing illogically to a holistic vision of the topic. The analytical teacher may describe peak-to-peak highlights of the topic, assuming that the students can logically fill in the missing parts. In either case, closer attention to the step-by-step, linear-logical approach makes the difference, as long as visual aids are used all along the way.

The outstanding result of holistic education is that the small group of highly visual individuals, who normally have difficulty in classroom environments, become more proficient with linear-logical, analytical thought processing. Conversely, the small group of highly analytical individuals, who often end up with unexplained school problems, become more proficient with holistic, configurational thought processing. And, the vast majority of eclectic individuals who have and orchestrate both propensities in blended thought processing are also assisted in this enhancement.

Teaching Students How to Think? It is questionable that educators CAN teach their students how to think, as so many say that they can and do. Students already know how to think. Some are analytically and others are visually oriented. However, in the context that *holistic education helps all students to benefit in both visual and analytical thought processing*, there is the intriguing possibility that properly nurtured, visual learners can become more analytical and gain proficiency in abstract sequencing and that analytical learners can become more visual. However, the greatest benefit from holistic education is that these strategies yield affective educational results as well (Santos Rego, et al., 1987). Students not only learn more in these classes, they enjoy learning.

On Becoming Holistic Educators. The task at hand in teacher education is to assist visual (self-directed) teachers toward becoming more proficient in presenting subject matter and at making verbal, linear-logical descriptions of visual aids. While these are largely the strengths of analytical (authoritarian) teachers, most of whom are well adapted lecturers, some of these individuals may need assistance toward being sensitive to students, whether or not they are comprehending the concept being presented. More efficient and effective use of visual aids and illustrations is another skill to be enhanced in teacher education.

The teaching of science is most conducive to holistic education because of the wealth of tangible teaching strategies such as collecting and looking at plant and animal tissue, studying differences in leaves, seeds, insects and taking field trips. Whereas, in the teaching of social studies, language and mathematics, steeped in symbolisms and abstractions, it may be somewhat more challenging, though not impossible, to implement holistic education.

In either case, all teaching should include more hands-on activities and more illustrations and demonstrations. By implementing holistic education, more students gain in that they are not only more attentive, but more personally involved with the learning process. Students are motivated by success. It has been said that nothing succeeds like success. All people have a need to experience success and when they do, they continue to be actively involved in the learning process. It is when they meet defeat that they finally withdraw from active involvement with learning. They often feel that they are "too dumb" to learn and thus frequently assume a facade of "who cares?" or they may become behavior problems. The sad fact is that once they did care and once they were motivated. The point is that the needs of more students are addressed through holistic education – a common strategy, delivered by very different teachers, each without compromise of a preferred teaching mode.

Is The Lecture Method Acceptable? Are there conditions in which the lecture method might be effective? The answer is not clear. The lecture method can be most effective, totally ineffective, fruitful, or fruitless, depending on the circumstances upon which it is delivered. Thus, any teacher needs to be constantly aware of the students and gauging whether or not they are comprehending or in need of visual aids, or hands-on involvement. One can find at least some of these answers in the hemisphericity model. However, some of the adverse conditions existing in education should first be reviewed. The most remarkable reality regarding the question of teacher-effectiveness is that most teachers, often even disgruntled teachers, think of themselves as mankind's gift to education. A high degree of self-confidence and self-esteem is not only desirable, it is a necessity toward the achievement of personal gratification. However, our personal observations over many years of experience, observation and interviews conclude that many of our colleagues unwittingly partake in the self-indulging practice of lecturing without visual aids, which can best be described as *intellectual egomania*. Teaching can and should be an ego trip – but, with limitations and done in moderation.

Lecturing Is Acceptable if Holistic Strategies Are Employed. Because the lecture method is the most widely used and exemplified method of teaching, it is also widely abused. When talking, discussing, or lecturing on a familiar topic of great personal interest, care is needed to monitor continuously for the learners' misunderstandings and to explain misconceptions as the lesson linear-logically unfolds. Lack of care will lead to poor cognitive achievement and to the breeding of negative affective results. (See Chapter 17 for personal and professional hints toward 80 percent achievement for the students 80 percent of the time).

While we advocate 80 percent student-success, the teacher should become alarmed when ten percent of the students are left helpless in hopeless frustration. Sadly, it is not uncommon for these figures to be turned around to a ten percent student-success rate. Carelessness in being aware of the students' affective state is not only a disservice to the students, it is also a disservice to the employing institution and an affront to the profession. A salary is rendered for the purpose of the teacher's *teaching*. Teaching implies the two part process of *dispensing* the information and *comprehending* what has been dispensed. Within practical limits, which we set at 80-80 on the basis of prolonged experience in the classroom, student achievement is directly the responsibility of the teacher. Any group of students can learn just about anything if paced linear-logically, in a step-by-step manner, when abundant visual stimulation is supplied simultaneously and concurrently with verbal explanations—*holistic teaching*, by definition. Conversations with disgruntled teachers and people who are generally critical of public education reveal complaints about students who cannot spell, refuse to learn math, do not belong in an academic environment, should not be passed on, and should not be allowed to graduate because it cheapens the same diploma that is given to "bright" students. Frequently, the reason for these failures rest with teachers pitching the lesson only to the analytical students in the class with total disregard for the visually oriented students. Lecturing without appropriate visual aids is an unacceptable mode of teaching. Those teachers who persist in doing so should be counseled to change their methodology for the benefit of their students. If counseling fails to alter this behavior, they should be dismissed. An educational institution can and should enforce these criteria as minimum expectation from its teachers.

With respect to a high level of cognitive achievement as a criteron for effective teaching, we share the experience of having learned under and served with colleagues who were masterful at painting pictures with words. Comedians are apparently good at painting visual imagery in linear-logical context. Both hemispheres appear to be involved and this is in every respect and by definition, holistic teaching. Some teachers are likewise skilled in comical presentations—little or no visual aids involved. Thus, in making this fine line of supervisory distinction, care should be taken not to confuse this very rare teacher with the lecturer who administers blatant disrespect for visual learners. But, these teachers are the exception and not the commonplace.

Understanding of Hemisphericity Eliminates Misconceptions. A better understanding of hemisphericity could eliminate the logic that commonly leads to the narrowly conceived back-to-basics movement and to the implementation of special programs for the "gifted." The common presumption is that "bright and gifted" are synonymous with being "analytical." The most common flaw with participant selection to these programs is that one can find political motivation. Children of the local staff or board are frequently given priority. When tests or academic performance are used to select participants in these groups, then linear-logical students are selected and visual students are not. Other times, students are included because of their "personality factor." Any of these groups is to some degree plagued with problems but succeeds mostly because "giftedness" is a multifaceted phenomenon found in many fields. In music, art, con-artistry (conversation artistry), acting, descriptive writing, and in the wit and physical skills of athletics, for example, such giftedness is essential and evident. A visual student, active in *all* school functions and easily motivated, could be and is frequently included among the "gifted." For the typical visual student, however, poor academic performance is an accepted way of life. They are usually judged unacceptable and are wrongly excluded from participation in these programs. To put this thinking in proper leadership perspective, we share the observation that a disproportionate number of disgruntled teachers think of themselves as "teachers of the gifted" while in the same breath complain of being heckled and plagued with "all of these others that have no business being in an academic environment."

We offer the possibility that by understanding the role of hemisphericity as a determinant factor for individual differences, and *implementing holistic education with the purpose of teaching the total group*, many of the unfortunate misconceptions about teaching and learning will vanish. Fortunately, the movement is in progress and the sad, previously mentioned cases are diminishing. There is reason for optimism. Nowadays, even casual observations of existing elementary school "gifted" and "magnet" programs reveal a healthy implementation of holistic strategies, "real-problem" solving, and "hands-on" experiencing with the objective of motivating learning. If implemented for the masses, the same programs could very well eliminate the need even to seek out the so-called gifted students. When visual students are provided with an equal opportunity to learn, such as through holistic education, they perform as well as analytical students. Because of the multi-faceted nature of "giftedness," the need to use it for the purpose of segregation vanishes. As evidence for this, Santos Rego, et al. (1987) have found that holistic education provides an atmosphere for most students to experience the pleasure of total academic success—cognitive achievement with positive affective results.

The hemisphericity model remains on the pioneering edge of the educational enterprise. However, it remains for us now to determine the parameters of the hemispheric phenomenon through logic and reason. For example, while it has long been stated that the right hemisphere is the seat of visual thinking and that the left hemisphere is the seat of analytical thinking (in most individuals), logic dictates the possibility that some individuals, though few, may have switched hemispheres. If so, these data could uncover experimental error in the literature and could unfold new hypotheses for researchers in lateral dominance (ambidexterity, for example) to investigate. It remains further to attract meaningful research in neuroeducation, and specifically in areas involving the role of hemispheric preference/dominance in teaching and learning, metacognitive development, and learner awareness of knowledge aquisition. As with the "visual and auditory" rethinking, much finer tuning is needed to help foster meaningful implementation of the hemisphericity model.

The task at hand is to determine logically the implications of hemisphericity so as to open the door for further research. As more and more educators become aware of its implications and ramifications, parallel research parameters will continue to unfurl and provide analytical and visual researchers with more and more information to put to the test.

PART II

WHY AFFECTIVE EDUCATION?

Patty M. Ward, Editor

Though schools are expected to teach for affective results, just as they are to teach for cognitive achievement, much less attention is given to affective education. A major reason often cited for this omission is the difficulty in measuring affective results. However, this discrepancy should not preclude educating with expectations written for affective aims and objectives.

Through the years, disagreement has centered around which is more important—cognitive achievement or the attainment of affective results. We do not advocate the dominance of either. We do propose equal emphasis on educating for affective results.

Why educate for affective results? The basic tenents and theme of our message deals with newly discovered principles and concepts, such as WHY (Part II), how to PREPARE (Part III), how to DELIVER (Part IV), and how to EVALUATE (Part V) affective education.

Why be concerned with affective education? The lack of this commonplace concern leaves us a nation at certain vulnerability and risk (Chapter 4). The task at hand is to bridge the gap between the community and school in an effort to more effectively channel students into the business world or into further education (Chapter 5). Long have we paid lip service to the gospel of individual differences among students, yet do we, in the reality of every day teaching, address individual differences? This requires a better understanding of the needs of all students as individual learners (Chapter 6).

P.M.W.

CHAPTER 4

AFFECTIVE EDUCATION
AND A NATION AT RISK

Gary D. Taber

The criticisms recently leveled at the condition of American Education focus almost exclusively on the cognitive aspects of teaching and learning. Taber suggests that if meaningful improvements are to come about, they must take into consideration a meaningful application of affective education.

P.M.W.

The educational system in the United States has recently received a barrage of conflicting reports concerning the state of its condition. Some of the reports portray the public schools as being mired in a rising tide of mediocrity, as having lost sight of their commissioned goals and objectives, and as being weak in leadership. The system is criticized for not having the vitality necessary to meet today's needs, much less the challenges of tomorrow. Some do, however, see signs of a distant revival and renewal as greater attention is given to striving for excellence.

Many politicians have seized the opportunity to capitalize on their constituents' growing bewilderment and concern. At the same time, local school districts have been fighting a losing battle with such problems as rising costs, shrinking financial resources, and declining enrollments. Administrators are frustrated with the public's growing skepticism and loss of confidence in

their schools. From yet another front come the proponents of such movements as prayer in the schools, merit pay for teachers, and tuition tax credits
for non-public schools, each entrenched in their own ideology and well funded with resources for a long battle. These concerns, generated from such
a diversity of vantage points, have raised fundamental questions regarding
the role and capabilities of public education. However, although these issues and demands are ostensibly rooted in a desire to improve the quality
of public education, they have all too often resulted in smoke screens, buzz-
words, and political jargon rather than serious debate.

Among the many recent reports on American education, two of the most
extensive were *A Nation at Risk: The Imperative for Educational Reform*, a
study by the National Commission on Excellence in Education, and *High
School: A Report on Secondary Education in America* by the Carnegie Foundation for the Advancement of Teaching. Although conducted indepen-
dently and differing greatly as to scope, methodology, and conclusions, both
have identified what were perceived as major areas of weakness in American public education. Each prescribes steps that must be taken if we are
to continue to produce the educated public that is needed in order to face
the challenges of the future. Both reports identify needed reforms in such
areas as content, expectations, time, teaching, and financing.

Despite their different methods, approaches, and conclusions, both reports
share the common orientation in dealing almost exclusively with the educational aspects of cognitive achievement. From this limited vantage point
are spawned propositions for improvement resulting from raising standards,
updating programs of study, increasing the number of hours devoted to
schooling, increasing the amount of homework, and revising teacher training curriculums. Both studies fail to broaden their outlooks by considering
such aspects as student attitudes, feelings, or motivation. By failing to recognize affective education as a vital force in learning, the two reports leave
untapped a major resource in the total effort to provide quality education
in the public schools of the United States.

Because the major role of public schools traditionally is perceived as being that of transmitting the accumulated body of knowledge from one gener-
ation to the next, the emphasis on the school curriculum has been heavily
biased in favor of teaching facts and developing intellectual skills. The back-
to-basics movement of recent years is witness and testimony that the Ameri-

can public expects the schools to provide programs which stress the learning of facts and the mastery of basic skills.

This view was skillfully fashioned by former Vice Admiral Hyman Rickover, who became the conservative spokesperson for those with the view that "a school system performs its proper task when it does a first-rate job of equipping children with the requisite knowledge and intellectual skill for successful living in a complex society" (Alexander, 1976, p. 5).

In contrast, there has been a growing realization that a school curriculum that deals solely with intellectual skills is inadequate to meet the needs either of the individual or of society as a whole. Beatty (1969) charged that educators "have devoted almost exclusive attention to the intellectual and cognitive processes" (p. 74), while neglecting areas of feelings and emotion. In agreement with that position, Combs wrote that "our preoccupation with . . . information . . . has dehumanized our schools, alienated our youth, and produced a system irrelevant for most students" (Moskowitz, 1978, p. 9).

Clearly, there appears to be a developing understanding that an over emphasis on the development of purely cognitive skills may actually be harmful to students and society alike. Citing the impact on society as a whole, Campbell (1974) charged that "the impersonal society as described by writers today is propagated by schools which neglect the affective domain" (p. 13). On a more individual level, Livingston expressed the view that the concentration of most curricula on developing purely cognitive skills can be "detrimental if it ignores the student's emotional and creative side, the affective realm which is inextricably linked to the learning of cognitive skills" (Toffler, 1974, p. 253). Livingston goes on to call for a balanced approach to education which recognizes the need to deal with the students' affect, while at the same time developing their intellectual skills.

The work of such educational theorists as Benjamin Bloom, David Krathwohl, Bertram Masia, and others (see Bloom, et al., 1956), culminating in the publication of two handbooks on the taxonomy of educational objectives, introduced to educators a new vantage point from which they have been able to view the school curriculum and the teaching/learning process. "Bloom's *Taxonomy*," as the work is most commonly called, gave educators an organized approach to the identification, categorization, and description of three separate, but related, categories of educational objectives, i.e., the cognitive, affective, and psychomotor domains.

For more than quarter of a century, as the potential contributions of the application of Bloom's *Taxonomy* have become more clearly understood and appreciated, an increasing number of educational theorists have become aware of the role that each of the three domains play in the total education of the child. More and more educators have begun to question the effectiveness of traditional curricula and methods which have been designed solely for the teaching of facts, the imparting of knowledge, or the dispensing of information—in short, which deal only with cognitive education.

An increasing number of American educational theorists have come to recognize the need to include the affective domain in the educative process along with the cognitive domain. Citing the school's responsibility for providing opportunities for personal growth, Moskowitz (1978) maintained that "education should deal with both dimensions of humans—the cognitive or intellectual and the affective or emotional" (p. 18). This view was echoed by Magoon and Davis who asserted that "the process of education is vitally concerned with the development of values and attitudes" (Magoon, 1973, p. 112).

Stressing the need to go beyond purely cognitive goals, Lynch (1981) cautioned that although curriculum demands must be met, "we must never lose sight of human dignity. All too often the subject area becomes more important than the people to whom it is being taught" (p. 83).

Nevertheless, in spite of the evidence that it is not only desirable, but necessary, to deal with student feelings and emotions—i.e, with affective education—there appears to have developed a growing chasm which divides that which the theorists propose from that which is actually happening in the contemporary classroom. While the major theoretical groundwork for affective education has been laid, it appears that the theory has had little practical impact on the behavior of the classroom teacher.

Beatty (1969) stated bluntly that "the area of feelings and emotion is almost totally neglected in our current educational process" (p. 75). Likewise, Kirschenbaum and Simon concluded that "so much of our education forces us to deny our feelings, to distrust our inner experience" (Toffler, 1974, p. 264). Decrying the schools' continued failure to adequately deal with affective aspects of education, Rogers has charged that "as a consequence of this overstress on the cognitive, and of the avoidance of any feeling connected with it, most of the excitement has gone out of education"

(Moskowitz, 1978, p. 8). In like manner, Moskowitz expressed the opinion that the school's failure to combine affective experiences with cognitive learning, at least in part, explains why "many youngsters don't find the classroom a place where things that are important to their lives happen" (p. 19).

Although current literature provides ample justification for the application of affective education, the frontline practitioners—i.e. the classroom teachers—still have not developed an appreciation for the intricate relationships between feelings and intellectual behavior. Classroom teachers, preoccupied as they are with the immediate concerns and demands of the school, have seldom had the opportunity in preservice or inservice teacher education programs to receive adequate exposure to the methods and techniques of affective education. Fear of the unfamiliar, incomplete knowledge of the essentials of affective education, and a myriad of overwhelming and conflicting priorities have all conspired to prevent classroom teachers from employing affective elements to enhance the cognitive performance of their students.

As plans are drafted to improve the quality and effectiveness of the American public school, the recommendations and findings of such studies as *A Nation At Risk* and the Carnegie Commission's *High School* will be invaluable guides. Care, however, must be taken to guard against the pitfalls of relying exclusively on cognitive achievement as the end product of public education.

If meaningful and lasting improvements in public education are to be made, it will be necessary for educators to begin the difficult process of incorporating affective strategies into school programs. Failure to do so will severely hamper efforts to effect the fundamental changes and improvements in school programs that the public demands. The challenge to administrators at all levels is to create opportunities for teachers to learn about and utilize affective strategies that, together with cognitive approaches, will result in richer and more satisfying educational experiences for our nation's youth.

CHAPTER 5

BRIDGING THE AFFECTIVE GAP

Frank F. Montalvo

Montalvo's contribution has several messages central to the theme of our book. Among the most important is the fact that by the turn of the century, it is conservatively estimated that every one out of ten Americans in the United States will have Hispanic heritage and most will speak at least one of the many Spanish dialects. Also, while the scenario he paints is most commonly found in barrio and ghetto schools, the coupling of affective education with cognitive achievement is uniquely a lesson for any school district with an eye for improving the affective quality of the learning climate. My own thought is that even good schools can be better. A high level of cognitive achievement is not necessarily indicative of a positive affective climate. Indeed, experience tells us that in mathematics education, students more often than not end up with an avoidance complex, rather than the desirable positive affective stance. Montalvo provides a model for coupling the affective quality of instruction concurrently with student achievement in the cognitive skills. He states that good schools build

Adapted from Frank F. Montalvo, "Making Good Schools From Bad" in Make Something Happen, *Hispanics and Urban High School Reform, Volume II*. (Hispanic Policy Development Project: National Commission on Secondary Education for Hispanics), 1984, pp. 71-74.

bridges between the cultural values of the home, community and schools. As a result, parents become active participants in their children's education. Students respond by blossoming in this positive, affective climate.

P.M.W.

My contribution on the topic of *affective education* is not as a school teacher nor that of the administrator of a school, where the topic is more than likely to have its greatest impact. Rather, my point of view is that of an Hispanic "who made it" through a rather complex, demanding, and often alien labyrinth called our American Educational System. My point of view is that of a professional social worker who has witnessed too many Hispanic casualties on welfare rolls, in correctional facilities, and in mental hospital clinics, whose lives were short-circuited, mis-spent, or misappropriated too early.

Teen pregnancies, adults that are unskilled for employment, early involvement with drugs, gang violence, and the vicious cycle of poverty that breeds more poverty . . . I mention but a few of the common social problems that are often associated with a history of low achievement, high absenteeism and dropping out of school. Although there is neither an obvious, single cause nor an easy solution for these problems, they are deeply rooted in three mutually reinforcing environments of home, community, and school. Unraveling the riddle will require our attention in all three of the environments.

However, first things first. At the heart of the matter is the involvement of the young people, themselves: their values, wants, needs, and cares — their affects. The success of any program can only be measured in terms of the number of individuals that it has funneled into upward mobility. One must not lose sight of the fact that it is through individuals that any movement succeeds.

Parents Value Education and Want to Help. Typically, adolescents in high school are in the throes of searching an identity related to their past and at the same time struggling to initiate a connection with a vision of the future that many of their parents cannot provide. Few Hispanic parents who have not completed school themselves can advise and guide their children through high school — can advise them on what courses to take, how to prepare their lessons, what occupations to strive for, and what is required for college entrance and success. They now share with other parents the uncertainty of a rapidly changing economy that trumpets over and over that their children's future security rests on their preparing their child to become "computer literate," when many of them suffer the public shame of being considered "functionally illiterate." Communicating in the language of education and achievement is difficult enough. Now there is a new discourse that they are told they have to learn. I have been told that 75 percent of future jobs will be computer-related. Hispanic parents see on television that three-year-olds are playing with keyboards, that grade school children solve their math problems on home terminals, and that college students drop out of college because their parents didn't provide them with computers. What is the message that Hispanic parents are receiving about their role and responsibility to help their children succeed?

I recently had the unpleasant experience of observing and then helping a mother to buy a computer keyboard that had been put on sale. All she cared about was that it was affordable, $49.95 plus tax, and that it would help her son get through school. She had seen the television commercials and she did not want her son to fail. She was suspicious of the salesman who spoke of all the peripheral equipment that would be needed at additional cost. "That can come later," she explained to me in Spanish, as she held in her hands what she felt was her son's future.

I use this example, if somewhat dramatic, to illustrate the point that Hispanic parents do value education highly and will sacrifice to see that their children achieve in school, even when the requirements to succeed appear alien to them and when they are not sure what is required of them.

Hispanic Families--A Resource for Schools. I believe that the role of the Hispanic family is very important in securing the success of the child in high school. While Hispanic parents value education, they need help in organizing that value in terms of *how they can contribute* to their child's education. Middle-class parents know how to do this. They can articulate the school's short-comings; the ingredients of a good education, the steps they have to take to supplement their children's education, and even what attitudes and values that can be contested as not in the best interest of their child's development. These are knowledge and skills not readily available to many parents in Hispanic communities, but ones which I believe have a good deal to do with achievement. I should also add that the family is a highly valued institution in the Hispanic community. It behooves the school to capitalize on this resource.

The challenge to the school is to de-alienize its environment by reducing the social and cultural discontinuities between home and school. I realize that some schools can succeed without extensive parental involvement. I suspect, however, that when they don't succeed, the home-school connection is missing.

I had the opportunity to visit ten high schools in Austin and Los Angeles as a part of a Ford Foundation High School Program. The purpose of this program was to recognize and award inner city schools that were making a clear effort to improve the climate and quality of education. The schools that were succeeding best in their efforts to improve the education of minority children all made strong and extensive efforts not only to involve parents in the decisions and operations of the school, but to also provide them with instruction and training for their role as parents of high schoolers.

This was especially characteristic of three of these schools that eventually received $20,000 grants from the Ford Foundation (see Time, April 25, 1983, in which it was said that the program was stirring new hope in the ghettoes). These outstanding schools were cognizant of the cultural and social discontinuities that might exist between home and school and made efforts to bridge them.

For example, one of the schools had converted a classroom into a "Family Room," refurnished as a living room for parents' committee meetings and from which they conducted their school volunteer activities. It was a tangible and institutionalized link between school and home that not only facilitated their entry into the system, but symbolized the value that the school placed on their contribution.

Another characteristic noted was the extent of the efforts made to foster parental leadership in neighborhood networks—clearly an effort to insure ethnic and area representation. Emphasis was on small group meetings, rather than assembling all of the parents at once. Attendance and formal membership were de-emphasized. One of the schools made an intentional effort to diminish the boundaries between school, home and community by utilizing the high school parents' group to dispense cheese and commodities being provided by a local social agency. These groups were especially important to the agency because they were composed of white, black, and Hispanic parents in a community that was undergoing ethnic and racial transition.

OBVIOUSLY, it is up to the school to build the bridge to the home and community. The cooperation of the parents provided a very important model for their children. It was a reinforcement of their parents' valued role in school, a positive contribution toward their children's self-image. IT IS ALSO OBVIOUS that the greater the discontinuity between home and school, the more the children will perceive the educational environment as alien.

Schools as Safe Havens, Not Prisons. The schools we visited generally provided bridges to the home. They also created a safe haven for students. . . a bridge over troubled waters, if you will. In marked contrast to some of the communities in which they were located, the award-winning schools had climates of order and purpose, with more interpersonal harmony than most of us expected to find. There was also an increased and focused approach to teaching, an emphasis on basic skills, and a balanced concern with both vocational and academic students.

Nevertheless, the first order of business for these schools was to provide for the safety of students and teachers. While these schools were all well fenced and monitored to secure the school for teaching and learning, principals and teachers visibly welcomed the students to school. Attendance in school and in class was a priority concern. The parents quickly got the message that the school was functioning well and was safe for their children.

I think that a school, attentive to these and similar needs, is one that encourages students to remain in school. Herein lies the heart of the matter. The students are encouraged and assisted in becoming more involved in their own growth, development, and fulfillment. In such a school setting, students develop a positive attitude toward school and education. When permitted to assume some responsibility in their educational planning and treated with respect, students are led toward becoming responsible and caring adults.

Teachers and Principals. It was repeatedly and dramatically emphasized at these schools that many teachers are not prepared to teach students from diverse backgrounds. Such teachers, who were insensitive to students' special needs and their individual pace, who were unwilling to extend themselves beyond the classroom and to modify and improve their approach to teaching, had to leave. While success in the cognitive domain can be measured in terms of student achievement, it was the quality of the individual teachers' contributions in immeasurable affective terms that sustained these programs.

One school, among the highest rated in the Ford Program, had replaced 85 percent of its teachers. This required autonomy on the part of the principal and support commitment on the part of the district administration to withstand the political pressure that followed. Equally impressive was the fact that once it was learned that the school was serious about improving the standard of education for its 98-percent minority student body, they were flooded with requests from teachers wanting to transfer to that school. The result? Ninety percent are continuing their education after graduation at this school. Indeed, it is worth herein noting that CBS presented the docudrama of this man in the two-hour Movie of the Week, "The George McKenna Story," starring Denzel Washington (Dr. Phillip Chandler on "St. Elsewhere"). For many teachers, teaching remains a calling and a challenge. But, they have to be convinced that the community and the central administration value the education of their children, and are willing to back it up with money and resources.

With or without resources, it was evident that the successful schools looked to themselves to improve both the cognitive and affective qualities of instruction, that they had to expect more from themselves in order to expect more from their students. Teachers had to turn in lesson plans to the principal every week; the principals, in turn, had to become instructional as well as administrative leaders. They had to review and discuss area-wide test scores and how math and language arts can be improved in all the courses taught. They had to plan for and demand, if necessary, workshops to renew their teaching skills. They had to institute programs for advanced students in math and science in order to stretch student expectations, no matter how small the classes were initially. At the same time they had to spend time initiating "adopt a school" projects with the business and public service com munities in order to enrich the program and to meet the special employ-ment and training needs of other students. They had to involve students, parents and themselves in improving the physical facilities, which mean so much to students and their pride in the school. They had to devise ways of keeping unwed mothers and fathers as well as juvenile probationers in school. Somehow they had to keep trying, because their trying meant that the kids would know that they cared, and the students would care about their education in return. The success of the program was instantly evident from the measure of individuals pressed into upward mobility as a quantity measure and by the spirit of the program as a measure of the affective quality.

The Evidence of Affective Education. To the students I talked with, it was the teacher's caring about "what they did with their lives" that was most important. The students were willing, in turn, to abide by dress codes, at-tendance standards, and to remain in school, and thereby, enrich themselves.

For students, "caring" was operationalized by the school and the teachers in arrangements for morning and afternoon tutoring by teachers or by other students, by counselors helping them with personal and family problems, by evidence of their cultural heritage displayed and discussed in class, by arrangements to secure the school and keep it clean and in repair, by ex-pecting them to attend class, and by encouraging them to see beyond their own world views. Affective education had been implemented by the teachers and the cognitive achievement of the students soared.

My sense was that affective education had been institutionalized, in so-ciological terms, in the form of "caring" on the part of the teachers and in the students with the resulting "pleasure and enjoyment" that simply cannot be measured. Affective education was firmly implanted, not solely an ac-cidental relationship between a teacher and a lucky student. I recall how lucky I had felt in my own life that certain adults took a special interest in me and advised me in ways my parents could not. These students were telling me that in a good school, caring was less a matter of chance and that it was a teaching skill and attitude that was valued.

The schools I visited were highly successful: not by absolute standards of achievement on state and national tests, nor by attendance records, nor by merit scholars, nor by having the best football teams. They were recog-nized for improving the quality of instruction, for raising expectations, for

instilling hope and pride in their students and their families, and for measuring success in terms of individual accomplishment. They were turning
things around because they understood that schools are also people . . . they
are family.

Some say that high school is too late, that the taste of success should
begin earlier. This may be true. However, I also know that for many Hispanic
children, high school is the last chance that they have. Many of them in
the schools I visited were making the most of it.

CHAPTER 6

MEETING INDIVIDUAL DIFFERENCE NEEDS: A KEY TO AFFECTIVE INVOLVEMENT

Rex L. Leonard and Patty M. Ward

In Part I, the chapters describe education in general and hemisphericity as generally implied in teaching and learning. In this chapter, the reflection is on WHY one should be concerned with affective education. The focal point of this response is on the learner as an individual.

P.M.W.

Affective education is the result of education with the attainment of affective results, as well as satisfactory performance in cognitive achievement. Education which addresses these minimum standards could lead to greater student achievement. As a result, learning could become a pleasure and the students made to feel good about themselves, thereby developing in each a positive self-concept. Affective education, simply stated, is that education from which the *students derive pleasure and joy*. If students are achieving successfully, the level of affective attainment is usually positive, or at least neutral, but rarely negative.

When assessing a lesson in progress, one must look beyond cognitive achievement, alone, as the end product. *The pleasures displayed by the students* are the best indicator of their enjoyment of the process. In the case of more complex situations such as mathematics and language, particularly English, there can be no pleasure derived if the student is not mastering the content at the time it is being presented. This has important implications for the teacher, as well as for the entire educational enterprise. In order to insure that the student masters each concept that is presented, at the time it is presented, the teacher must thoroughly explain each step of the way, supported with ample visual and media assistance, as needed. It is at this point that a lasting impression can be made if the learner applies the concept in a real problem. Such an application also gives the teacher a way to determine if the concept was mastered. Next comes the decision to reteach, or to go on to the next concept. Depending on the age of the students, the teacher may need to keep the instruction simple so that each important aspect of the lesson is not lost in the verbiage.

In the case of mathematics education, it might be well to use manipulatives when appropriate. For maximum success, delivery is best done in small segments with the expectation of at least 80 per cent achievement by 80 percent of the students, on each segment of the difficult concepts. Minimum expectation for teachers might extend further. Effective instructional management requires the recording of the achievement test items missed, which items are missed most frequently, and an analysis of which steps were missed when taught. Achievement of less than 80 per cent should be interpreted as unacceptable. To increase the level of effectiveness, the concern must include not only WHAT concepts were missed most frequently, but WHY, with the focus being on the TEACHING PROCESS. Such questions as these can be helpful in making the proper professional adjustments: Can the visual aids be improved? Can the logic of the explanations be improved? Was there too much delivery, too fast?

That's old hat. Every teacher already knows HOW to conduct a lesson toward the achievement of minimal instructional management expectations. However, some may CHOOSE not to put this standard into practice, not realizing a need to do so. It is for these individuals that we offer, what is hopefully, a convincing explanation for the need to do so. Traditionally, teaching was practiced with little or no concern for individual differences AND/OR the learning process. The teacher had no need for concern beyond a personal knowledge of the subject matter. However, with a better understanding of individual differences among students, and teachers alike, should come ample reason for the necessity to adjust one's thinking in accommodation to this knowledge.

What's new, in the advent of hemisphericity, is the fact that students have different learning styles which require different approaches and that holistic strategies effectively deliver instruction to this diversity. Our purpose is to help teachers, who also have hemispheric diversity, to accept holistic educational strategies as THE NORM toward the more fulfilling success of 80/80 achievement—80 percent achievement—80 percent of the time.

In essence, our task is to explain WHY holistic strategies are successful. To do so requires the understanding that hemispheric diversity among teachers dictates the need for visually oriented teachers to be student-centered and analytically oriented individuals to be subject-centered (see Chapter 3). This does not mean that one teaching mode is superior to the other. It simply means that different teachers have different internal needs that are outwardly expressed in philosophical differences. These differences are as natural and normal as day and night, or as one being a blonde and another a brunette. The visual teacher is best suited for self-directed instructional management. Analytically oriented teachers are best suited for authoritarian instructional management.

However, it should be noted that this diversity in actual practice is most pronounced among highly visual and highly analytical teachers. In that the vast majority of teachers are eclectic, that is in hemispheric terms, they have both visual and analytical propensities and blend freely from both, self-directed and authoritarian modes. It is pointed out that in order to understand the vast majority in the blended middle, one must observe the pure forms at either end of this diversity (as discussed in Chapter 3). We are reminded here that prior to hemisphericity, there was limited success in the evaluation of teaching and learning as separate entities.

Today, we can evaluate the teaching act for its own level of effectiveness with respect to student achievement in both cognitive and affective results. Further, the teaching act is recognizably a separate and distinctly different activity than the learning act on the part of each individual student. The teacher has access to and can react to the statistical results of the group achievement, in general. This information has traditionally been the guidepost for those teachers who were concerned with elevating student achievement.

However, today the concern which we emphasize is based on the fact that visual learners are in need of a different mode of instruction than analytical learners and that holistic strategies effectively address both learning styles. Holistic strategies assist visual learners by providing ample visual stimuli. They assist analytical learners, as well, by providing linear-logical and analytical discourse. The added effectiveness is that holistic strategies assist visual learners in becoming more analytical by dealing effectively with the linear-logical discourse and they assist analytical learners to become more effective in their visual thought processing. All students prosper in that each becomes more proficient in both visual and analytical processing in their everyday thinking.

In conclusion, educators often say that they can teach their students "how to think." This is probably a misconception in that students already know how to think from birth, some being visually oriented and others being analytically oriented. However, if through holistic education, visually oriented students can indeed become more proficient analyzers and analytically oriented students can become more proficient visualizers, then an educator could truly be teaching students "how to think!" The most incredible outcome, however, is so latent and subtle that one must be reminded of how effective and well the affect has been served.

PART III
PREPARING AFFECTIVE EDUCATION

Rex Leonard, Editor

The broad range of phenomena involved in affective educational practice makes defining the concept challenging. The concerns that typically identify this area of education encompass an interest in students as persons, i.e., their mental health and personal development, as well as their social skills, roles in society, and the all-encompassing expression, "joy in learning."

Educational systems respond to the demands of the society they serve. However, rarely do they seem to be agents of change. With society's present demand for personnel with technological and scientific skills, our schools and universities have geared themselves to respond to the requirements of supplying professionals, technicians, and skilled laborers. As a result, instruction has largely been in the cognitive domain and testing, as a part of that instruction, has followed suit. Diagnosis of the best learning mode of students has not played a major role, nor has achievement in the affective domain been given wide attention. The assumption has been that all students learn cognitive materials in similar ways and teaching practices have embodied that belief.

The potential of affective education could be realized rather quickly through the use of holistic education. It depends on teachers electing to use holistic strategies in their classrooms. However, the long term potential will depend on the type of accomplishments planned and carried out by the educational community. Aside from the dedication to holistic education, there appears to be great potential in a number of areas in affective education – mental health, interpersonal growth, values education, and group development for solving the pressing problems of schools. Affective education, in its many dimensions, can be viewed as a stategy comprehensive for change.

Implementation of some of the precepts of affective education in the classroom can be found in this section. If educators are at times confused about why affective education is important, it may reflect a need for more understanding of conditions that are conducive to learning for affective behavior (Chapter 7). Studies contained in this part provide clues as to some of these deficiencies among unsuspecting teachers (Chapter 8). The use of more encompassing goals in implementing affective education may provide some answers. There are herein suggested some sources for more information and guidance concerning the preparation of typical lessons that more adequately involve student affect (Chapter 9) and more specifically, judgemental decision making (Chapter 10).

R.L.

CHAPTER 7

CONDITIONS CONDUCIVE TO AFFECTIVE RESULTS

Patty M. Ward

As a teacher of emotionally disturbed students, as a licensed counselor, and as a professional educational diagnostician, Ward has had the pleasure of working with many students, parents, educators, and other professionals in an effort to provide the best possible education for students. It would be impossible to work in these capacities and not be aware of the need to educate for affective results. She is committed to more humane goals and objectives at all educational levels. Grades should not be a deterrent to learning, but an indication of achievement or the challenges to improve.

R.L.

Pressures that abound in today's world also impinge on students. Parents experience pressures from the work environment, from lack of work, the high cost of living, marital problems, and health problems, to name but a few. It is my experience that students are not spared the agony and frustration that their parents' experience in trying to cope with such problems, and unfortunately, a large number of students come to school weighted down by problems that many adults would find overwhelming.

It is essential that the school environment be a humane one—a haven—a place of safety in which one is free from hurt, at least intentional hurt. Given the amount of time students and teachers spend in the school setting, dare we strive for anything less than a humane environment?

Such an environment is a prerequisite to educating for affective results. However, a humane environment does not just happen. It requires a commitment and organization toward that end. Teachers and administrators play the major role in determining the climate in the school setting, and certainly in educating for affective results.

The authoritarian, self-directed and eclectic teachers are discussed elsewhere in this book. Any of these teachers can be equally effective in creating conditions which are conducive to affective results—if the commitment is there. Some students profit from the more restrictive environment of the authoritarian teacher—such as the student who lacks self control. Other students benefit more from a less structured environment, such as that of the self-directed teacher. Generally, all students profit from exposure to a variety of environments over the years. Regardless of the type of teacher, however, the humane environment is essential.

In the humane environment the student is respected as an individual, treated with empathy, given encouragement and expected to achieve. For this to occur, however, the teacher must know the student as an individual—as another human being, in order to sense individual needs, whether they be academic or emotional. There are times when the student simply needs a little individual help to master a certain concept, or task. At times the student just needs someone to listen and offer a few words of encouragement. One might need the benefit of an adult's wisdom or guidance. Unfortunately, one can never be certain of the kind of assistance that a student needs, or how great or even desperate this need is. It is probably the lack of this understanding that has resulted in complacency. At times the affect seems to belie the depth of despair that a student is feeling. The uncertainty, the fear or the despair may not be obvious. Far too many students are unaccustomed to expressing these feelings. One can never be sure what has happened to that student in the past or immediately preceding contact with the teacher or administrator. This is precisely why there is a great need to treat each student with kindness, understanding and patience. Why risk being the "final straw" that causes another human being to either explode or to give up completely? Is it not far more humane and more profitable to offer encouragement?

Everyone needs encouragement. Students need it just as teachers need it. We all perform better with encouragement. If there had not been many kind and encouraging teachers along the way how many of us would continue to set goals?

As a teacher of emotionally disturbed students, I repeatedly observed the value of positive expectations and encouragement as motivating factors for students to perform academically and behave appropriately. The years of experience leave me convinced of the value of positive expectations and encouragement. Basic to these factors, of course, is caring about the student and communicating this to them.

The students that came to me had failed terribly in regular education. After a great deal of time and effort it was apparent that these students needed more individualized attention than the regular education classroom could provide. They received little positive feedback at home because they were usually in trouble at school, and this caused problems for the parents. I used the most common strategy—that of communicating to them my belief that they were worthwhile and capable. I then provided opportunities for them to be successful—each in their own way, each at their own rate.

In time, they began to feel good about themselves. Nothing works like success. Their beginning success fostered more success. Every person feels a need to be loved and to be successful. They were no different.

I am reminded of a student who was diagnosed as emotionally disturbed and legally blind. He usually came to school hungry, sometimes ill, and often with bruises. My first impression was that he belonged in a class for the visually handicapped, but was assured that he was, indeed, in the appropriate class. I inquired if I might expect him to perform similar to others in my class and was assured that I could, with certain modifications.

So I began to teach him. When we got to manuscript writing, he would become extremely frustrated. He had difficulty forming some of the letters. When erasing he would make a hole in the paper which brought on tears. He then would spit on it, throw it on the floor, stomp on it and have a tantrum.

However, I knew that he could do it. To allow him to do less than what he was capable of doing was, and will always be, unthinkable to me. I provided him with a warm and nurturing environment, lots of enthuiasm, and expectations that he achieve to the best of his ability. With much positive reinforcement and success, he eventually got beyond manuscript and the tantrums but unfortunately, never beyond coming to school with bruises.

I often grieved over the situations in which my students existed. There were those who were hungry, neglected, or physically abused. The greatest consolation, during those years, was in knowing that for a brief period of time, I could provide a safe place—a place where each was a worthwhile human being—a place where each could succeed.

Expectation that every student achieve to the best of his/her ability is a key factor which favorably influences affective results. A problem sometimes arises when every student is expected to achieve the same thing, at the same rate, and in the same manner as every other student in the class. The teacher may cover the material and even finish the textbook. However, it is quite likely that several have not learned what was presented.

Students come to school with different abilities and achieve different levels. They learn at different rates and have different styles of learning. *Each can learn, but not all in the same way*. Expectations for all to learn are most important, but must be coupled with the appropriate modifications for individual differences, when needed, if mass learning is to occur.

Grading is another area of great concern to students and sometimes a cause of great distress to them. They are usually as concerned about grades, or more so than teachers. It is unfortunate that at times the student associates poor grades with self-worth. The manner in which evaluation and feedback take place is very important. Imagine the impact on one's self-concept if one continually receives papers which are covered in red marks—especially when those around are getting back papers with As, gold stars, or the like. Is it not more valuable to provide feedback along with the paper? Would it not be of even greater value to plan for remediation? It has been my experience that it is much more beneficial to reteach or remediate on an individual or group basis at that point and then allow the student to demonstrate competency of that concept, rather than just giving back a paper full of red marks and a score recorded in the grade book and proceeding on to the next concept to be taught. (Chapter 17 provides teachers with a way to determine and achieve more success with more students.)

Just as students have different academic abilities and needs, so they have different emotional needs. The establishment of rapport between students and teachers is very important. It is extremely important that there be someone with whom each student has established rapport and trust.

I am reminded of a lovely girl of about fourteen years of age who was referred to me for evaluation due to poor academic achievement. She was very quiet and cooperative, and never caused anyone any trouble. She had only been in this particular school a few months. Her P.E. teacher was presenting a unit on sex education. After one of the sessions she asked to speak with the teacher in private. (Imagine the tremendous trust that had been established, for her to share her concern with another person.) Her problem was of the magnitude that probably would overwhelm many adults. She had been trapped in an incestuous relationship with her father for several years. It was her fear of pregnancy that prompted her to trust this teacher with her problem.

The important point is, that the school had a counselor and other professionals, but she turned to a teacher. How fortunate that such a person was there with whom rapport and trust had been established. It is frequently the caring teacher to whom the student in need turns. Many schools do not have counselors readily available, and without a caring teacher, there may be no one to whom the student in need can turn.

Upon request, I recently worked with three students in a small school which had no counselor. The first student's problem was that his step-mother had told him that if the father died, as they expected he might, she would put him in an institution for children with behavior problems. Imagine being concerned, at 13 years of age, with having no one that wants you. His mother could not provide for him, neither *emotionally nor financially*.

The next student that I saw was experiencing guilt feelings because his friend had attempted suicide. The friend had confided in him, but he had not really believed his friend was serious. After his friend failed in his suicide attempt this student felt extremely guilty because he had not told someone. I was later informed by his teacher that several years previously, he had witnessed his father murder his mother. At this particular time he was regressing academically. He talked of feeling as though he had no friends. When reprimanded by a teacher, he felt that all of the students were laughing at him. When asked how he dealt with these feelings, he said he put his head on his desk and if he were outside, he walked off alone.

The third student was a small girl who came in, twisting and wringing her hands. She began to sob. She told me that she wanted to see her mother, but her mother had been killed by a hit and run driver the previous month. Though it is not always the case, all of these children were living with someone other than natural parents. I was told that there were numerous other students with problems, but these were the ones the principal felt needed immediate attention.

I am convinced that too often adults are unaware of a child's need to express feelings, of a child's deep need for comfort. If these needs are unmet in the home and the school, where are they met? What happens if they are not met? What happens if there is no safe place?

As a person, I have grown because of the difficult times in life; I have been able to survive the difficult times because of those with whom I shared my joy, my sadness, and my concerns. As a person, an educator, a student, I am well acquainted with the feelings which range from eager anticipation, pleasure, and joy, to anxiety, frustration, and despair. It is the encouragement during the difficult times that provides all of us the strength to persevere. Because I care that there are those students for whom there may be no safe place—either at home or at school, I am compelled to ask—for whom do schools exist?

CHAPTER 8

THE AFFECTIVE DOMAIN: A STUDY OF TEACHERS' PERCEPTIONS

Renato A. Schibeci

How do teachers regard affective domain objectives for a science curriculum? A study by the author of the views of science teachers in Western Australia provides some clues to these perceptions. Over two hundred science teachers replied to a mail survey which sought their views regarding the objectives (both cognitive and affective) of the science curriculum which they were teaching. In addition, 35 teachers were interviewed individually so that a more detailed picture of their views could be obtained. A comparison of the responses on the questionnaire indicated that the views of teachers interviewed were not different from those who were not interviewed.

The main result of the mail survey was that cognitive objectives were rated more highly by the teachers than were affective objectives. This general result was probed more deeply in the interview phase. Although the interviews with the 35 teachers were unstructured, at some stage the teachers were asked two questions: Are student attitudes important? Are they assessed? It is important to note that teachers were given the opportunity to present their views as fully as they wished. As they had already completed a highly structured questionnaire, it was considered essential to provide them with the opportunity to present a wider perspective on issues relevant to science-related attitudes than was possible through structured questions.

An analysis of these interviews is presented in two sections, corresponding to two categories of affective domain objectives. The first relates to *attitudes to science* (such as "enjoyment" and "satisfaction"). The second relates to *scientific attitudes* (such as "tolerance of the views of others" and "suspended judgement").

The Teachers' Views - Attitudes to Science. The teachers generally said that they regard student enjoyment of science lessons as very important. Whether students actually do enjoy their science lessons, however, is a different issue. One teacher thought that "the majority of students are just going through the routine of being in a subject." Another said, "they are eager to get into it, but when they find that science is not just fizzing and bubbling, but there is a lot of writing of exercises, they start to lose a bit of interest."

All teachers interviewed believed that the student attitudes to science generally deteriorated during the high school years. One teacher summarized the views of his colleagues in this way: "Oh yes, I think they are keen to do anything at year 8. God only knows what we do to them between year 9 and 10!" A number of factors related to this decline were mentioned by different teachers, including: "As students grow into adolescence, they become interested in a variety of non-school activities," "Low-ability students do not achieve well, and so lose interest," "Too much emphasis is given to achievement measured by cognitive tests," and, "The home environment is not conducive to positive attitudes to science."

Thus, on one hand enjoyment is regarded as an important objective; on the other hand, students do not seem to enjoy their lessons after their initial flush of enthusiasm. What factors, according to the teachers, influence student enjoyment of science lessons? Teachers regarded their own attitude to the science topic as an important influence. Thus, some biology teachers did not find physical science topics such as "heat" and "mechanics" very interesting and felt that this dislike communicated itself to students. One teacher stated:

> Last year I was interested in the topic "Mice and Men" because the kids love animals. . . I was interested, they were interested. We had 86 mice running around and they thoroughly enjoyed it. . . It was super, it was good. On the other hand, "mechanics," I can't stand.

Teacher enthusiasm (either for a specific science topic or for science in general) was consistently mentioned by teachers as being an important influence on student enjoyment of lessons.

Another factor mentioned was the amount of practical work students did. This may, of course, be linked to teacher enthusiasm. A teacher interested in a topic may make more effort to provide practical activities related to the topic. There was general agreement that students enjoy such activities. In the words of one teacher: "Mainly, I think they seem to enjoy the practical work. . .they love heating things up and melting them down." Another interesting comment on practical activities was provided by one teacher:

> Boys expect to work with their hands, whether it's fixing up the car or butchering the meat or whatever; but girls are not expected to do these things and. . .they have got this attitude built into them that, here we are, this is a science room, science is difficult, I can't do practical things.

Whether this comment applied to practical activities in biology lessons (which girls, according to the teacher, generally enjoyed) is not known.

Teachers indicated a number of ways in which students' interest in science could be improved. The most frequently mentioned of these was "relevance." The claim was made that interest in science would be fostered if the science program was made more relevant, "by the encouragement of student inquiry," "by the discussion of issues raised by students," and "by the study of areas nominated by students."

Two of the teachers interviewed disagreed with their colleagues' views of the importance of attitudes. They said that attitudes are irrelevant and if students are interested and enjoyed their lesson, this is to be regarded as a "bonus." Another cautioned against making science enjoyable to its own sake: "If you simplify (concepts) beyond a certain point in attempting to make science enjoyable, I think a lot of the times the concepts are lost."

While the majority of teachers believe that student attitudes are important, they all indicated that no formal attempt was made to assess student attitudes since they had neither the expertise, nor the time for this type of assessment. All teachers interviewed believed that they could gauge student attitudes quite well through informal methods. In the words of one, "I have a fair idea of each individual kid's attitude and I think that enjoyment of science is an indication of a job well done."

Some teachers believed that attitudes could not be assessed in the same way as cognitive achievement. Many believed that attitudes should not be used in formal assessment, as in this statement: "I don't think you should use it (an attitude mark) as part of their assessment. However, it could be useful in knowing how to react to the student." There was a general disquiet about the use of attitude data for grading purposes. This disquiet, however, was generally not well articulated.

The Teachers' Views - Scientific Attitudes. Teachers' views of scientific attitudes revealed a degree of confusion. For example, one teacher said: "I believe they (scientists) are no more open minded than anybody else, and probably less so." No distinction is made between the behavior of the scientist in his/her professional and non-professional life. These scientific attitudes are best regarded as professional standards, not behaviors of any individual scientist. It was clear, however, that this view was not held by many of the science teachers interviewed.

Since the teachers interviewed did not have a clear, coherent view of "scientific method(s)" and scientific attitudes, students are left to interpret in their own individual way the cues emitted by the teacher (for example, the way the teacher conducts a demonstration lesson in science, or the way in which the teacher presents experimental results). Thus, students must acquire scientific attitudes individually if teachers, on their own admission, do not make conscious attempts to inculcate such attitudes.

Despite the lack of clarity about scientific practice, teachers believe that (in the words of one of them) "the scientific method should come through science lessons." In the light of this, a comment from another one of the teachers is interesting: "I will be honest. I often cheat the results at times on long-term experiments purely because if the experiment doesn't work (the students will say) our teacher is useless because the experiments don't work." Does the scientific attitude "honesty in reporting data" need to be modified in school science?

Teachers were not optimistic about the possibility of their students gaining scientific attitudes. There was a general view that the ability level of students was an important factor. One teacher summed this up by saying: "In A-level (high ability) kids we try to develop the attitude of inquiry and open-mindedness and flexibility in their thinking. This is not possible with basics (low-ability children)." This same teacher, however, agreed that the development of an attitude of inquiry was the overall aim of the curriculum. Another teacher believed that children already have an attitude of inquiry, but only on some topics: "Kids have an attitude of inquiry. You talk to them about sex — they have a tremendous attitude of inquiry but it is only inquiry into things that are motivating them." Some teachers doubted that students' level of thinking was sufficiently developed to allow these attitudes to be fostered.

All teachers interviewed indicated that no attempt was made to assess these attitudes formally. One pointed to time as the problem. "Time is at a premium and questions related to scientific method are very time-consuming and one doesn't seem to get much reward from them." It may be, however, that the lack of a coherent view of the role of scientific attitudes may be a more important reason. The assessment of attitudes to science was regarded as being somewhat ethically repugnant; this objection was not raised with the assessment of scientific attitudes.

Teachers interviewed indicated quite clearly that they made no systematic attempts to teach towards affective objectives. Professional and biographical characteristics of interviewed teachers suggest that they are a representative sample of their colleagues. This implies that little attempt is made to implement all aspects of the science program specified in the curriculum guides.

Review. This study of perceptions of science-related attitudes supported the hypothesis that science teachers regard cognitive objectives as more important than affective objectives. It also revealed that science teachers are not only confused, but are also unable to articulate their views. What is important, however, is that teachers' lack of clear thinking on these issues is a reflection (at least in part) of the confusion shown by curriculum writers in this area. These findings on attitudes indicate clearly the vagueness and inconsistency displayed by many of these writers. These findings are also consistent with the confusion in the literature on attitudes to science.

It is clear that curriculum writers need to provide much clearer guidance on the role of, and justification for, science-related attitudes. Perhaps scientific attitudes can help students in ordinary life, even though some writers have cast doubt on this view. Nevertheless, because there is not sufficient agreement among curriculum writers, science teachers are expected to implement a set of objectives which are plagued with practical and ethical problems, without the benefit of guidance.

Curriculum writers and and developers need to be more aware of teachers' perceptions of affective objectives. While teachers may share the view that attitude objectives are important, they certainly (from their own reports) do not systematically teach towards attitudes. Rather, they teach towards students' acquisition of knowledge. A clearer justification for attitude objectives is needed, together with guidance for teachers on how these objectives can be achieved and assessed.

Teachers' reported lack of attempts to teach attitudes directly leads to a number of questions. What kind of attitudes are students acquiring? Are these attitudes acquired mainly outside the science classrooms? What classroom process variables are most closely linked with students' attitudes? Unfortunately, despite the wealth of literature on attitudes in science, we are unable to point to any clear answers to these questions at present.

Whither Attitudinal Objectives? A general, basic assumption of curriculum writers and researchers is that we can change attitudes in the desired direction. This assumption may be examined empirically. In one study, the effects of teaching strategies on racial attitudes have been investigated and the researchers found that mean racism scores were lowered in experimental groups, while they rose in control groups. However, the investigators reported that in every group (experimental and control), some students moved in each direction. That is, even when teachers deliberately set out to moderate racism, some students become "more racist." These results are disturbing. The authors believed that the results would be similar for attitudes toward school subjects. They concluded that "however deeply a desired attitude is valued, the teacher cannot expect to win every student in a group toward it."

Student achievement with cognitive objectives appears to have led curriculum writers, unreasonably, to expect similar success with affective objectives. There is some evidence that teachers have realized some of the difficulties with attitudinal objectives, although their thinking has not been particularly coherent, nor were their views well articulated.

This chapter is not an argument for the abandonment of attitudinal objectives in science or in any other curriculum area. It is rather designed to alert curriculum writers to the danger of assuming that attitudinal objectives may be treated in the same way as cognitive objectives.

There appears to have arisen a vague assumption that attitudinal objectives are a "natural" part of a specification for a science curriculum. This assumption needs to be examined more critically by curriculum writers than has been done to date. The selection of appropriate affective objectives is an important activity. A much clearer, explicit justification for inclusion of attitudinal objectives needs to be provided, both for curriculum and research purposes.

CHAPTER 9

ENVIRONMENTAL SCIENCE PROGRAMS PROMOTE AFFECTIVE RESULTS THROUGH HOLISTIC EDUCATION

David R. Stronck

Holistic educational strategies contribute either positively or negatively toward the success of any educational program. However, with environmental education, the results are generally positive because of the usual concern for the preservation of our living surroundings and other topics of universal interest. While the traditional subject-matter disciplines have mostly emphasized the development of a cognitive understanding, environmental education goals usually call for a change in attitude, philosophy, and/or behavior.

Educational goals have traditionally emphasized cognitive achievement with an almost total disregard for affective results. These are concerns in the *cognitive domain*. However rarely, one can find from time-to-time an emphasis on attitudinal goals and a concern in the *affective domain*. When both *cognitive* and *affective* goals are coupled in a single lesson plan, as are so often the case in environmental education, the strategy is most likely to implement holistic education. Environmental education may well have been a primary force towards helping teachers to better understand affective educational objectives and affective achievement through *holistic educational strategies*.

In that positive affective results should be based on a rational understanding, environmental education emphasizes the holistic approach by leading the students from a cognitive understanding to the organizing of a system of values. In that holistic educational strategies can either promote positive or negative results, it is crucial for the instructor to monitor the results of a given lesson to make sure that it remains positive from start to finish. For example, if the subject matter is presented in a way NOT UNDERSTOOD by students, they end up frustrated, with a negative attitude, and have an unwanted dislike for that subject.

The very nature of the environmental concerns lends interest in each lesson toward the achievement of positive results. However, this has not been the case with the traditional subject-matter disciplines. Many are the concerned teachers who have helplessly observed negative affective results in their students and ultimately the dislike for that subject-matter. Teachers of these other subject areas can learn much from the observation of a well coordinated environmental science program where through holistic strategies, there is substantial cognitive achievement, PLUS the promotion of affective results.

The most commonly accepted definition of environmental education was included as a part of the Environmental Education Act of the 91st Congress (1970)

> . . . "Environmental education" means the educational process dealing with man's relationship with his natural and manmade surroundings and includes the relation of population, pollution, resource allocation and depletion, conservation, transportation, technology, and urban and rural planning to the total human environment.

Marland (1971) described a holistic approach within environmental education:

> Environmental education is directed toward attitudes, and, therefore, the emphasis is on process and not content. . . Environmental education is not a new subject, for we have taught about the values of conservation for many years. But we now see environmental education as a new approach to learning. Even as the attitudes of individual worth, free agency, democratic consent, and cooperative effort are learned subconsciously in many parts of the public school curriculum, so must

new attitudes of environmental concern pervade each subject, each course, and each discipline, ...

How to Include Affective Goals. The back-to-basics movement has recently emphasized the need for evaluating students according to clearly defined objectives. However, the stated goals rarely opt for or list the securing of affective results. Many teachers may be avoiding the teaching of affective goals simply because they do not see how to evaluate these results for grading purposes. For example, if students display a negative attitude or concern toward a particular environmental issue, they may be demonstrating a different set of values from that of the teacher and not necessarily ignorance nor an unreasonable attitude towards the topic. In a democracy we must guarantee the right of each citizen to his opinion and set of values. Because many aspects of environmental education seem to conflict with attitudes found in some of the American subcultures, teachers may easily justify a policy of avoiding, and thus omitting these issues from curriculum.

On the other hand, students everywhere have been demanding greater relevancy. The high dropout rate from high school among teenagers is often related to boredom. Through the media of television, radio, and the press, students are generally aware of the existence of major problems. For example, the meltdown of a reactor's core in a Soviet nuclear power plant has generated intense interest among young Americans in the debate over the use of nuclear power. These students are puzzled by the attitudes of teachers who refuse to relate topics of their courses to the real world of conflicts and values.

Kohler (1966) called for meeting the contemporary dilemma by fusing philosophy of science, value and fact into a meaningful system. First of all, teachers should attempt to meet the dilemma by deliberately writing out desirable goals in the affective domain. According to the levels of this domain, the students can be encouraged to progress from mere awareness of problems to the formulation of a value complex. Teachers can explain the levels of the domain and their expectations for students' progress and achievement. The greatest difficulty may arise from the fact that teachers must carefully assess the students' responses according to stated criteria and cannot mechanically grade students on the basis of giving back "the right answer."

The following table allows teachers to keep a record of their students' progress through the levels of the affective domain simultaneously with consideration of each topic provided by the Environmental Education Act (see Figure 9.1). A checkmark may be used to show the attainment of a level on the scale of the affective domain. No checkmarks may indicate no willingness to consider a topic. The advantage of listing all topics from the Environmental Education Act is to assure an adequate recognition of the major problems now facing the nation:

RECORD OF THE LEVEL OF STUDENT PROGRESS
IN THE LEVEL OF AFFECTIVE DOMAIN

TOPICS OF ENVIRONMENTAL EDUCATION	LEVELS OF THE AFFECTIVE DOMAIN					
	1	2	3	3	4	5
Conservation						
Pollution						
Population						
Resource Allocation & Depletion						
Technology						
Transportation						
Urban & Rural Planning						

FIGURE 9.1

Many teachers stress that their students must get "the right answer to questions." In the affective domain, the emphasis is teaching the clarification of values without having one set of right answers. Roths, Harmin, and Simon (1966) offer the following guidelines for teaching values:

> Don't moralize, no matter how subtly, during value discussions. Do avoid 'yes-no' and 'either-or' questions, for both limit value-related thinking. Avoid 'why' questions for they push children who have no clear reasons for choice to make up reasons for choices for the benefit of the question. . . . Don't worry unnecessarily about parents. . . . Do get into sensitive areas, important areas, as soon as you dare. . . . Don't try to give the students grades on the basis of what they say, for that will squelch honesty faster than almost anything. . . . Do include many 'you' questions. . . for that is the essence of the value process.

Although teachers must avoid assessment during value-clarification discussions, they can use the usual means of evaluation during activities of the cognitive domain. There is a practical overlap between activities emphasizing cognitive achievement and those stressing the attainment of affective results. The interrelationships are especially obvious in the higher levels of these domains. For example, the cognitive activities of analysis and synthesis are required before one can do the affective act of organizing one's values into a system. The cognitive work of evaluation presumes the existence of a clear set of known criteria, in much the same way as the affective level of characterization by a value or value complex presumes the possession of a clear set of values. Holistic education calls for the coupling of cognitive activities with affective goals.

Teachers may begin by providing information and problems in the cognitive domain. They may also grade the students in the usual manner. Nevertheless, the conscious effort to specify affective goals will add relevancy to the direction of the instruction. The students will then be encouraged to use knowledge gained in the cognitive domain to support a value system. This value system should evolve from information and be based on logical and consistent reasoning. Teachers are not indoctrinating when they are encouraging students to make judgments and form values on the issues that are considered. The outcome of the students' personal decisions is not predetermined. The ultimate goal of environmental education is a well-informed, aware society intelligently planning its future. The democratic ideals accepting various cultures and attitudes can be preserved especially through encouraging goals and activities that promote affective results.

Project Teaching and Affective Results. Watkins (1926) recognized the advantages of assigning projects:

It seems probable that project teaching insures attainment of more aims, gives greater possibility of learning in general, should induce better learning "growth," insures increased expenditure of effort on the part of pupils, develops greater initiative and independence, gives greater opportunity for "socialization," teaches pupils to think for themselves and develops the "problem solving attitude," encourages a wider range of reading, provides better for the needs of pupils of varying capacities, and provides better opportunities for real and genuine teaching, and for teacher growth than in traditional types of teaching.

In the same year, Garber (1926) described the superiority of project classes over nonproject classes in terms of both achievements on standardized tests and the expression of preference by the students. Nevertheless, the schools did not widely accept projects as a major instructional technique.

In the 1960s the introduction of many new curriculum programs, especially in science, seemed to reduce interest in promoting projects and to emphasize laboratory instruction in cookbook format. In the 1970s the environmental education movement encouraged the current views and use of projects. This insight suggests that the environment in which the students live contains many problems that are in need of prompt solutions. The Department of Health, Education, and Welfare (1970) observed:

> A program of environmental encounters, through both school and nonformal activities, leads to personal involvement with environmental problems or situations. . . . A simple and conventional encounter would be a study and work trip to a stream or other natural area.

The following are some examples of appropriate projects posed by environmental questions:

1. What is the relationship between trees and air pollution? Can planting trees reduce air pollution in your town?

2. What is the relationship between birds and insects? Can constructing bird houses reduce populations of insects in your town?

3. What areas are preserved for wildlife in your region? What are some of the advantages of having such wild areas? Should some local areas be allowed to go wild?

4. What kinds of transportation are most efficient, economical, and healthy? What should your town do about promoting the use of bicycles?

Such activities are not only relevant, but promote both holistic and affective results. Students are led from activities of the cognitive domain to those of the affective domain. The key to success is the teacher's ability to identify local problems that will capture the interests of the students.

Conclusion. The environmental movement has attempted to provide holistic education through the simultaneous provision of objectives in both the cognitive domain and the affective domain. Unfortunately the projects suggested by environmental education are often neglected because of recent emphasis on the back-to-basics movement seeking rigorous evaluation and academic achievements. Nevertheless research has demonstrated for over 60 years that the use of projects would increase academic achievement as well as providing important skills of self-directed learning.

CHAPTER 10

A COGNITIVE-BASED PROGRAM CAN PROVOKE JUDGEMENTAL STUDENT DISCUSSION IN A HOLISTIC EDUCATIONAL EFFORT

Frank F. Montalvo

Hispanic workers are widely under-represented in child welfare programs throughout the country. Further, there is an insufficient number of bilingual-bicultural workers available to serve Hispanic clients in the forseeable future. This situation requires that the primary goal of educational institutions in human services, particularly child welfare workers, initiate emergency measures to recruit Hispanics into their programs.

Meanwhile, Hispanic clients continue to be served by non-Hispanic workers. While the services are helpful, they are mostly rendered incomplete, inappropriate, or unresponsive to the needs and interests of the Hispanic population. Those who are marginally acculturated and in need of the most comprehensive services are often least served. Thus, a program is needed which will have an appreciable impact on large-scale service systems. It is to be cost-effective, easily delivered within the organization to large numbers of workers throughout the state or region, and relate directly to child welfare practice.

Adapted from Frank F. Montalvo, Tonia T. Lasater and Nancy G. Valdez. "Training Child Welfare Workers for Cultural Awareness: The Culture Simulator or Technique," Child Welfare League of America 61(6):341-352 (June, 1982). The Culture Simulator.

An Interim Step. In view of the preceding observations, it seems that developing effective methods of training child welfare workers about cultural values and beliefs would provide an interim step toward improving child welfare services to the Hispanic family and community. The program herein presented was an attempt to meet these requirements by using an innovative training technique that presented familiar casework situations in a self-instructional, problem-solving form. The critical difference in these casework situations was that they included a cultural variable that influenced the interaction between the worker and the client. In the process of solving these incidents, non-Hispanic child welfare workers showed significant improvement in their learning about the Mexican-American culture.

I describe the development of these materials, the strengths and limitations of the training instrument, and its potential use in training child welfare workers for cultural awareness. In the evaluation of our program, teaching modules composed of 40 casework incidents were developed, along with an accompanying trainer's manual.

The Culture Simulator. The training instrument or technique is known as the culture simulator, which is composed of a series of written vignettes or scenes that simulate a problematic cross-cultural incident created by the differences in values, beliefs, or lifestyles between a Mexican-American client and a child welfare worker. The instrument is an adaptation of the technique that has been used to train multi-national business people and educators teaching abroad (Fielder, et al., 1971).

The incident is followed by a question that focuses on the client-worker interaction that took place. Four multiple choice answers are provided as realistic alternative explanations for the transaction. The reader is then instructed to choose the best of the four answers and read the corresponding rationale, which explains why the answer selected is or is not the best alternative available. He or she continues selecting answers until the best alternative is confirmed by the rationale. Rationales for the less-than-best answers provide an opportunity for correcting misconceptions, stereotypes, or ineffective interventions, which are often good casework or counseling techniques but are culturally inappropriate. The rationales for the best answer explain the nature of the traditional value in question, and suggest more culturally responsive and effective casework approaches to the situation.

The rationales are therefore the key teaching elements in the instrument.

The following vignette taken from the published instrument, the Mexican-American Culture Simulator for Child Welfare, illustrates the technique.

The Open Door. Mrs. Gonzales cheerfully greets Mr. Sanchez, her child welfare worker, in the reception room and they begin chatting about the rising price of gas and food. In the office they continued talking and laughing about the humorous television programs they had both watched. As they talked, the caseworker made a move to close the door which did not shut entirely. As he did so he acknowledged Mr. Gray, his supervisor, who was walking by.

During the supervisory conference later in the day, Mr. Gray raised the point with the caseworker that the office is a place of serious business, and friendly visiting is inappropriate in a professional casework relationship. Mr. Sanchez questioned the supervisor's interpretation and explained that:

A: Mary Gonzales and he have both a friendship and a professional relationship.

B: Perhaps Mr. Gray was envious of the ease with which he was able to establish a relationship with ethnically similar clients.

C: This was his way of introducing more sensitive subject matter into the interview.

D: This informal, personal exchange is an important part of their relationship.

If the worker selected answer A, that the individuals had personal as well as professional ties, he or she would turn to the rationale with the corresponding letter and read the following:

Rational A

If there happened to be a previous personal relationship, it is likely that the caseworker would have questioned, on professional grounds, the assignment of this case to him. Please re-read the vignette and select another answer. (7 percent)

The rationale informed the worker that he or she did not select the best answer and addressed the issue of controlled objectivity in professional relationships.

The percent score provided at the end of the rationale informs the reader that 7 percent of child welfare workers taking the test form of the simulator also selected that answer. The precent figures are added to the final module constructed to pique the reader's interest and provide the worker with an incentive to read the rationales that were not selected. This aspect of the instrument is discussed later in this article.

If the worker selected answer B, he or she was instructed on two important issues in minority intergroup relations: that cultural awareness can be taught and that the worker's ethnic similarity by itself does not guarantee understanding of clients from different socioeconomic circumstances.

Rationale B

> It is true that culturally compatible relationships are essential for providing effective services. However, ethnic similarity is not a sufficient condition in view of social class differences that exist between many workers and their clients who have the same ethnicity. Also the fact that cultural understanding can be learned by ethnically different workers questions the implication that Mr. Gray could not be understanding of Mexican-Americans. Such differences among workers can sometimes become a source of tension in the office, but there was not any clear evidence of this in the vignette. Try again. (4 percent)

Selecting answer C indicated that the reader interpreted the exchange of pleasantries as a way of putting the client at ease, even though the nature of the client's problem was not mentioned, the client did not appear to be upset, and such behavior might be interpreted by the client as a delaying tactic on the part of the worker if the subject matter was indeed sensitive. The rationale was worded as follows:

Rationale C

> This is a plausible reason, although there was no mention of the nature of the problem in the vignette. There may also be more appropriate methods of putting the client at ease that do not risk being

interpreted as avoidance by the client. Try again. (4 percent)

Answer D correctly identified la plactica as a culturally relevant and appropriate exchange between individuals in the Hispanic culture who are involved in a business or professional transaction. The individuals do not have to be on close personal terms to engage in such activities.

Rationale D

> The informal chat, or plactica, serves to build trust and confidence. In the Mexican-American community, such informal discussions usually precede and follow business and professional transactions and serve to establish rapport and respect. This process facilitates negotiations. You should never view the platica as a waste of time, but rather as an integral part of the interview. Good choice. Please continue to the next vignette. (85 percent)

This particular vignette illustrates the building of relationships with Mexican-American clients. The rationales showed how the instrument can take advantage of the opportunity to teach about casework relationships, interviewing techniques, and intergroup relations, as well as the intended purpose of teaching about the culture. Vignette construction also provides subtle reinforcement of themes or lessons learned earlier, such as the mistaken assumption that the worker's ethnicity guarantees understanding. In a subsequent vignette the worker who misunderstands the client has a Spanish surname.

It is a basic principle in constructing vignettes that the worker in the incident exemplify good casework practice and be presented in a postive light; poor practice or negative attributes confound the results and discourage the trainee's involvement and identification with the worker.

There is also a danger that the trainees in search of guidelines may overgeneralize from the new information and learn "new stereotypes," such as the notion that all Mexican-American families are of the extended type. Careful construction of vignettes, answers, and rationales can minimize this risk by varying the circumstances under which certain values prevail and under which they do not. For example, in one situation the father is presented as the head of the household; in another his authority is limited; and in a third the wife assumes responsibility for negotiating with outsiders. Teaching about the circumstances under which different values operate is an important strength of the culture simulator.

Commonly held stereotypes associated with Mexican-Americans, such as machismo, fatalism, submission to a "culture of poverty," and passivity, are dealt with directly and their sources explained in the rationales.

Other vignettes in the teaching module include cultural values and customs related to folk medicine and religious beliefs, family relationships, family pride and obligation, bilingualism, and particularly sex- and age-related roles. Most of these values are presented within a child welfare context, involving such issues as child abuse and neglect, adoption, foster care, and planned parenthood.

The Use of Traditional Cultural Values. The vignettes do not purport to teach the trainee about the total distribution of values and beliefs that exist in the community, nor about the extent and depth to which they are held. Rather, it aims to teach child welfare workers about the more traditional or core values that are related to the family and are held by many Mexican-Americans.

There were four major reasons for taking this approach. First, there is the issue of relevancy for practice. Most clients who receive assistance from child welfare agencies are living near, at, or below poverty levels. Traditional orientation tends to be associated more with urban and rural poor and migratory workers than with those in higher socioeconomic levels who have experienced a greater degree of acculturation.

Second, there is the training need on the part of child welfare workers. Those who participated in the study reported being most concerned and ignorant about the traditional values that are held in the community and the reasons why they are held. They were less concerned about misunderstanding the more acculturated clients who were more similar to themselves. They also believed that the impact of minority status on clients was an important issue to understand, but that it should be treated in its relationship to cultural values, for example, in differentiating between the relative influence of poverty and culture on individuals and their families.

Third, the ability to transfer knowledge to other Mexican-American communities in the Southwest is important. Core values are less subject to regional variations and tend to be shared by individuals from different locales. Only those values about Mexican-Americans that were identified in the general literature from different parts of the United States that were verified by local informants were used in the vignettes.

Fourth, there is the utility of the vignettes for other Hispanic groups. As a project that was funded by the Children's Bureau because of its potential for national significance, the authors were attentive to the module's adaptability for use by agencies serving different Hispanic communities. Traditional values, such as personalismo, and customs, such as folk medicine, are generally shared among Hispanic groups. The available literature on Puerto Rican and Cuban values was also examined. Some were cited in the references and integrated into the analysis of vignettes in the trainer's manual that accompanies the teaching module.

The issue of acculturation is an important one in the Hispanic community, although beyond the scope and intent of this training. It is addressed in a number of vignettes in the module, although less than the subject demands. Nevertheless, it should be noted that no one individual adheres to all the values in a given culture. Socialization is seldom complete. Rather, each person represents a configuration, profile, or pattern that is unique to him or her. The values, beliefs, and customs represented in the module describe some basic touchstones of the culture, but do not define it or a given individual. This training is intended to be only a beginning for those who have a sincere interest in serving the Hispanic community.

Source of Vignettes. Critical casework incidents were identified in 30 group interviews, conducted in Spanish and in English, during 1980 with 180 key informants from low-income Mexican-American communities in San Antonio, Texas. The informants were identified and selected by six community service outreach agencies that serve the barrios. It is important to note that while an extensive review of the literature about the Mexican-American and Hispanic experiences was conducted in preparation for training field interviewers, the primary source of information for the instrument was derived from the life experiences of the community residents.

The field interviews and the development of the case materials were conducted by the project staff with the assistance of 17 experienced child welfare workers from the Texas Department of Human Resources. Thirteen were Anglo-Americans and 4 were Mexican-Americans; 13 were female and 4 were male. They were arranged into two research groups, one of which had an equal number of Anglos (4) and Mexican-Americans (4), and the other was composed of 9 Anglo-Americans. Ten days of training over a 3-month period included information on Anglo-American and Mexican-American values, field interviewing, and developing and constructing vignettes and rationales.

These tenured workers were specifically selected to participate because of their knowledge of agency policies, administrative procedures, and the standard approaches to child welfare practice. The group was weighted toward non-Hispanics in order to include their perspective in identifying and analyzing cross-cultural differences and similarities and because non-Hispanic child welfare workers were to be the primary recipients of culture simulator training. On ethical grounds, the staff was also sensitive to avoid descriptions and explanations that were offensive, however subtle, to either ethnic group. The project staff was impressed with the interest, dedication, and enthusiasm exhibited by the field interviewers throughout the project.

Evaluation. A total of 40 vignettes and 160 rationales were arranged into four volumes in order to evaluate the simulator's training effect and to test for cumulative learning. Similar value themes were dispersed among the volumes, although their ease or difficulty to solve was not known. Three groups, with a total of 27 child welfare workers, undertook training with the teaching volumes. Three groups, with a total of 46 workers, tested separate volumes in order to determine whether the training groups' scores on a particular volume were due to reading previous volumes or chance.

As presently tested and constructed, the full teaching potential of the child welfare culture simulator has not been realized. First, the test form of the instrument presented the vignettes to the readers with the rationales deleted. When they returned the answer sheets with their selections, they were given the entire vignettes and scored their own answers before proceeding to the next of the four volumes. As a consequence, the effect of reading and learning from the rationales in the fourth and last volume was not tested with a new series of 10 vignettes. Thus, the effect of only 75% of the instrument, 30 out of 40 vignettes, was testable.

Another limitation of the culture simulator's present form involves the self-instructional procedure: only the rationales of the answers selected need to be read, as illustrated in our example above. The educational value of the rationales that are not read is lost. An alternative procedure under consideration, the principal author's development of a mental health form of the simulator, requires the trainee to read all the rationales and make an independent judgment of each before being provided with the best answer. The interim measure used here, providing the trainee with the percent scores obtained by his or her peers, relies on the reader's interest, curiosity, and competitiveness to read the other rationales in the vignette.

Even with the limitations in the testing and training procedures, the three training groups showed significant increases, varying from 16% to 25%, in their knowledge of Mexican-American culture. The increases occurred despite the relatively high baseline knowledge possessed by each group, from 42% to 55%, as measured by their correct scores on Volume 1. When prior knowledge was considered, the improvement rate became impressive. For example, the group that scored 42% correct on the first volume scored 67% correct on the fourth volume. The increase was 25%, but the rate of improvement from where they started was 43%, in that they obtained 25% of the remaining 58% needed to reach 100% (the test for difference in mean scores was significant at $p = .01$).

Test of the individual volumes with separate groups indicated that in each case the training groups' scores were significantly higher than those obtained by separate test groups on different volumes. For example, the highest separate volume score obtained by a test group was for Volume 4 with 47% correct answers. As mentioned, the training group referred to above scored 67% correct on that volume, a significant difference of 20% ($p = .05$). The lowest test group score was 24% on Volume 2, which compared to the training group's score of 52% correct on that volume. The conclusion reached was that the culture simulator developed cumulative learning for the reader where he or she transferred knowledge from one volume to another.

Among the more surprising results of the evaluation was the discovery that experienced, tenured workers with 6 or more years of practice did not score significantly higher than workers with less than 3 years in the field. The conclusion derived from controlling for years of experience was that the culture simulator tested for and taught cultural awareness more than it tested knowledge of casework technique or child welfare practice.

A recent review of practitioners' clinical judgments suggests that their decisions are difficult to modify even when contradictory evidence is provided (Montalvo, 1981a). Nevertheless, the simulator appears to create doubt in the trainees' preconceived ideas and assumptions about Mexican-Americans and seems to involve them in developing empathy for another's world view. These are among the important initial steps that Witkin suggested were necessary to alter perceptions and correct inappropriate practice decisions (1979).

The result of the simulator's initial evaluation were favorable and in keeping with the positive learning outcomes discovered by intercultural researchers using this technique (Landis, et al., 1976). It is not known, however, whether the knowledge gained will influence the child welfare worker's casework practice. This is a major weakness shared with most training programs and there is a critical need to develop criteria for evaluating the performance of workers trained with this technique.

Summary. The Mexican-American Culture Simulator introduces a new, cost-effective method of training child welfare workers for cultural awareness. It was published in 1981 by the Worden School as a two-volume module containing 20 vignettes each (Montalvo, et al., 1981b). The accompanying trainer's manual provides instructions for conducting modular training and a discussion guide that analyzes the values and practice implications in each vignette (Montalvo, et al., 1981c).

The simulator has a number of key advantages over some of the traditional seminar approaches to this type of training.

1. It is directly related to child welfare practice, providing information in a familiar problem-oriented casework format that facilitates the transfer of knowledge to job-related activities.

2. It enables the trainees to learn at their own pace, in private, and at a location of their own choice.

3. It exposes the trainees to standardized material, enabling them to assess their progress and controls for variations in the trainer's expertise.

4. It is brief and easily administered, thus allowing for its efficient distribution and use in training large numbers of workers.

5. It provides a baseline level of knowledge that can be supplemented with more extensive and specific training to meet differing staff needs.

Its principal disadvantage results from its apparent effectiveness and utility. There is the possibility that it might be used as the sole source of training for child welfare workers about the Mexican-American community whose cultural pattern is too rich, varied, and complex to be captured by a single instrument that focuses on cognitive awareness of selected traditional values. Within its limitation, however, culture simulator training introduces an interim method of improving services to the Hispanic community.

PART IV

DELIVERING AFFECTIVE EDUCATION

Craig A. Buschner, Editor

Affective education can be delivered by using a variety of teaching strategies in various disciplines. These strategies can be used across disciplines if adaptations are made. Examples are offered for instruction for delivery of affective education (CHAPTER 11), the training of social workers (CHAPTER 12), physical education (CHAPTER 13), and military instruction (CHAPTER 14).

C. A. B.

DELIVERING AFFECTIVE EDUCATION

Isadore L. Sonnier and Craig A. Buschner

With the exception of those efforts leading to the Graham and Heimerer (1981) discussion of "warmth," "praise," and "expectancy" as characteristically common dimensions among effective teachers, there is the lack of a substantial or definitive literature on specific methods and techniques that effectively deliver affective learning. We discuss our views and offer plausible suggestions concerning the pioneering of this uncharted territory of education. The reader is reminded of our premise that holistic education is a function of hemisphericity (see Chapter 2) and as such, provides fertile ground for students to attain positive affective results (see Chapter 3). In that hemisphericity is herein regarded as the foundation for holistic education, it follows that the principles of hemispheric preference may be fundamentally regarded as the basis for those methods and techniques that foster positive affective results. With these precepts in mind, the delivery of affective education is suggested to depend heavily on *the nature of cognitive achievement with positive affective attainment* which in turn depends on *teacher-student-subject matter interactions that are not only conducive to, but contribute to a healthy delivery of affective education.*

The Nature of Cognitive Achievement and Affective Attainment. While those processes and procedures of successful and effective cognitive achievement are well documented in the educational research, it is not so for the nature of the student's affective attainment. Much is known about ways to effectively raise the quantity of student achievement. However, little is known about maintaining a positive level of affective quality in the learning environment. When more is learned about measuring the quality of teaching delivery, it follows that more will also become known about how to improve the quantity level of cognitive achievement.

We point to the implementation of holistic education as a set of teaching strategies with the potential for delivery and maintenance of a respectful level of both cognitive achievement and positive affective attainment. As educators come to appreciate this holistic vista of teaching and learning, they will develop their own skills in the fostering of positive affective results for their students.

Positive Affect and the Different Teaching Modes. Another view we share is the probability that a learning environment with happy and enthusiastic students is with little doubt attributable to a happy, reflective and responsive teacher. Further, this concern for the quality of the students' affective attainment levels can be accommodated by both analytical and visual teachers. Understandably, analytical persons usually perform best and more comfortably as authoritarian teachers and, as such, have a primary concern for students' cognitive achievements. Visual persons, on the other hand, perform best and more comfortably as self-directed teachers and will usually show a greater concern for the attainment of positive affective results. We quickly point to the probability of error in any attempt to correlate and stereotype "teacher happiness" with any one of the "teaching philosophies" or with any particular hemispheric preference. However, the revelation that hemispheric preference is a basis for many of the human characteristics does indicate a more natural flow of teacher and student happiness in the self-directed teacher's classroom. Although there is also an indication that the authoritarian teacher must make an added effort to obtain and maintain happiness as a quality of affect among the students, the fact of the matter is that many do.

We inject at this point that there is a set of strategies that enhance teacher effectiveness, with little added effort, for both visual and analytical teachers. Holistic education has the potential for effectively delivering both of these parameters, quantity achievement with a positive quality of affective attainment, in a substantial number of students. While more data is needed on teacher effectiveness with holistic education, there is reason to believe that regardless of philosophy, teachers will gain personal satisfaction in this favorable level of student accomplishment. Any teacher can be fulfilled with the pride and joy of satisfactory results when the students perform and display a substantial quantity of cognitive achievement, coupled with a positive quality of affective attainment.

Hemisphericity Enlightens a Better Understanding of Teacher-Student-Subject Matter Relationships. Can teachers get to know more about their students through a better understanding of hemispheric preference? While little is known and even less of this reality is established pedagogy, there are certain consistencies that emerge. For example, there can be little doubt that visual learners achieve most effectively when taught by visual teachers. Conversely, analytical learners achieve most effectively when taught by analytical teachers. However, because of the limited understanding of hemispheric preference and the lack of a widely implemented and practical application of holistic education, time, experience, and research in this parameter are needed to determine its significance.

Our assumption is that the implementation of holistic education will significantly foster a better relationship between students and teachers. While cognitive achievement will continue to be the most important criterion for teaching effectiveness, the quality of that learning, here-to-fore ignored, can be measured and will become a more prominent criterion of teacher evaluations (see Chapter 17). It is strongly suspected that teacher-student-subject matter relationships will gain prominence as a criterion for teacher evaluations when it becomes better understood that the positive or negative nature of this relationship lies squarely in the hands of the teacher.

Teacher-student relationships are herein presumed to rely heavily on the students' success or failure in academic performance, both on an individual and on the class-group level. In that holistic education has the potential to improve the academic aspects of student-performance, it follows that through its implementation, teacher-student-subject matter relationships will likewise and conspicuously take a positive turn.

Delivering Affective Education. Delivering affective education has the appearance of being dependent on the implementation of holistic education. The reader is reminded that holistic education is achieved when discussing a point, visual aids are appropriately and adequately displayed, simultaneously and concurrently with the explanations. On the other hand, visual stimuli, it appears, can be most effective when thoroughly and linear-logically explained. Educators have long known that words alone are rather an ineffective tool of education, unless accompanied with visual stimuli. Time and familiarity with these suggestions will determine their appropriateness to change these points in the delivery of affective education from postulates to pedagogy.

CHAPTER 12

AFFECTIVE INSTRUCTION IN CROSS-CULTURAL SOCIAL WORK EDUCATION

Frank F. Montalvo

As in the curriculum of other professional training programs, affective attainment in social work education consists of that fuzzy area of teaching and learning that deals with interests, sentiments, feelings, attitudes, values, awareness, judgement, openness, commitment, and risk-taking on the part of both students and teachers. It is difficult to measure and evaluate this quality of learning, or to deny the existence of favoritism when one attempts to use such non-objective measures to evaluate student progress. It is much easier and safer to add up scores, derive means and standard deviations, and to assign grades than to pass judgements on student progress.

Minority students and students from lower socioeconomic backgrounds are weary of the objectivity that is practiced by institutions that "go by the book." They suspect that the inflexible rules which rule out individual differences do not serve them but function to cover indifference; as some say "equal opportunity is seldom equal." Meanwhile, students overhear ethnocentric remarks made by graduating straight-A students and shudder at the prospect of such students someday administering programs that will continue to rely on the victims to solve social problems (Ryan, 1971). An objective system allows this to occur.

Adapted from "Cross-Cultural Social Work Education," *Journal of Education for Social Work* 19:48; Spring, 1983.

In the professional training of social workers, failure of the school to consider affective attainment in social work education also leads to neglect of the realities of practice with minority clients, a disproportionate number of whom are poor. Indeed, it may even discourage cross-cultural practice.

Affective vs. Cognitive Learning. Students quickly discern the style of learning that is valued and rewarded. All too often, the learning environment fosters a cognitive learning style in response to the authoritative, pedagogical approach that teachers tend to favor. The emphasis is on ideas, the written word, appeal to logic and reason, and the search for the optimum model and the most elegant solution. This teaching style encourages emotional distance and a relative stance toward the students' values.

By contrast, in cross-cultural practice the student will become embedded in the sights, smells, and sounds of the cultural life of the people—their customs and styles of interaction, their eating habits, social pace, and language—aspects that are subtle, subjective, deeply felt, and envelop their lives. The worker's assumptions and values are challenged repeatedly by the most trivial events. The problem is compounded by the necessity for the practitioner to make decisions and accept the consequences of these decisions. The commitment to act on one's values is vital, but it precludes an objective, relativistic stance toward competing values.

The initial enthusiasm and euphoria of learning, displayed by many students, soon buckle and give way as confidence dissipates and competence is questioned. Some experience guilt and overcompensate in dress, manner, and supposed insights into the minority experience, only to have their purpose and role in the community challenged anew. They may withdraw into their office, feel confused, irritable, and frustrated, and begin to harbor feelings of resentment toward community residents.

The accumulated strains of meeting the demands of everyday practice in an unfamiliar and threatening environment is aptly described as an experience of culture shock (Brislin, 1981). The less the student is prepared for this affective confrontation, the deeper the disabling reactions will be felt and the longer they will last. Perceptive students may sense this danger and as a result may be prone to avoid a commitment to cross-cultural practice.

What students often overlook is that the adjustment process is an expected, situational, and transitory response to cross-cultural adaptation, and not necessarily a revelation of bigotry and deep-seated racism. Such reactions cannot be totally prevented, but they can be managed in order to develop the emotional stamina needed to deal with the high degree of stress that is experienced. Students can be helped to develop greater personal and cultural self-awareness, to learn new response repertoires, to acquire new knowledge and skills, and discover new social realities that are hidden from most casual observers (Adler, 1975). To most students, the trust that clients give them is in response to their deep empathic understanding. As a result, the sense of competence and feeling of satisfaction they experience in doing well are the stuff and reward of social work practice.

In any curriculum designed for the human services professions, which include among others, teacher education, it is important that students have an opportunity to develop self-awareness and insight into their own affect, particularly those feelings regarding intergroup relations and poverty. At the core of this affective-cognitive dilemma is the need to help students to develop a rational approach to ordering, evaluating, and measuring their own affective attainment. The framework for allowing this to occur is open discussion, initiate conceptualization, and invitation to scrutiny.

Evaluating Affective Attainment in Instruction. Although evaluation of affective delivery is discussed elsewhere, one cannot be sure of ongoing effectiveness without ongoing evaluation. The process of delivery has guideposts for this ongoing and built-in evaluation technique. The model used by the author is a modification of Krathwohl, Bloom, and Masia (1974), who view affective development along three dimensions: *becoming receptive* to, *becoming responsive* to, and *increasing valuing* of cross-cultural knowledge, experience, and practice. Each dimension or stage includes roughly progressive learning phases. As a heuristic conveyance, the model should be thought of as the interweaving of these stages and not as disjointed behaviors.

Becoming Receptive. The student's willingness to attend to and take in information about the minority experience and about themselves in relation to that experience forms the basis of becoming receptive. Students tend to move in their receptivity from more cognitive and peripheral concerns to more attitudinal and central ones. The three important phases in the stage of becoming receptive, detectable as positive or negative behaviors, are awareness, openness, and immediacy – "bringing it home."

Receptive students are aware of the complexity of cultural group experiences and are open to the personal implications for themselves as learners. They often see facts as less relevant than people's perceptions and attitudes. Receptive students will also note more similarities than differences between groups but will find that the differences are important. The process of becoming more receptive is similar to Shulman's (1979) "turning in," or developing preparatory empathy. Students may experience discomfort, uncertainty, and at times confusion while coping with information and feelings.

Among the negative expressions, unreceptive students will flaunt boredom and state correctly that minority and majority groups are similar in basic needs and life goals. They also point to similarities and commonality, not to bridge differences, but to reduce them to a common denominator. As a result, they devalue and dismiss unique features as inconsequential. These students may not be avoiding contact with the materials, but rather may be truly disinterested and have no stake in the field – at the time of the evaluation – but, may become receptive later. Patience is the treatment to this diagnosis.

Becoming Responsive. Becoming responsive has behavioral consequences, especially when the student accepts active involvement with minority content and people, and begins to "learn by doing." Becoming responsive means becoming more self-directed, more willing to expose weaknesses and vulnerability, and more enthusiastic in the active pursuit of knowledge and competence. The phases of this stage include complying, taking risks, and satisfaction – pleasure, zest, enthusiasm, and fascination with the profession.

We often encounter problems in assessing this stage of development in students. Learning about the psychology and sociology of racism and poverty is not a pleasurable experience in the usual sense. For example, learning that one's interpretation and response to a client revealed an ethnocentric bias is not gratifying. Yet, one can detect in the students' responses the thrill and satisfaction of being stimulated to discover more about themselves and a "new world" around them. They establish and maintain satisfying relationships with others in the work setting and enjoy the positive impact that they have on the lives of others.

Increasing Valuing. When students begin to experience satisfaction in their responsiveness to minority concerns, there is promise that their behaviors will begin to cluster around the cognitions and positive feelings often referred to as values (which can be negative). One of the guideposts to this stage of development is that behaviors become more consistent and stable as they are invested with sentiments and beliefs. Cross-cultural helping becomes valued. For example, it is felt to be worth pursuing in spite of declining government interest and funding, or only passive interest from teachers, colleagues, and peers.

The phases of this stage include acceptance of, preference for, and a commitment to the profession. Students accept the intrinsic worth of a multicultural orientation. Acceptance borders on blind or controlled faith. Conclusions are made and actions taken on incomplete or even unreliable information. And, with good instinct, intervention strategies turn out to be viable, satisfying, and durable, although they may lack proof and elegance. The student shows preference for this profession and values the cross-cultural training and work. The subject area is not only regarded as important, but it is actually sought out over others for study and practice. And, we have seen this commitment made against the wishes of parents, spouse, and friends. But, the student is convinced that national as well as personal self-interest are at stake in improving intergroup relations.

Summary. The affective attainment is as important in learning cross-cultural and minority content as the cognitive achievement for students of the social work profession. And, my feeling is that affective education is more important in all of the other areas of human development in higher education than is presently recognized. Continuing to ignore the affect because it is difficult to measure has serious consequences, most highly felt for those professionals in human services that end up in cross-cultural practice.

The model presented is a framework that has been found useful for ordering and evaluating students' progress in social work education at the Worden School of Social Work at Our Lady of the Lake University in San Antonio, Texas. However, further refinement of the scale, herein presented as various phases in each of the three stages of affective development, can be observed in students of social work. The model may be helpful in the training of students in other areas of human services, including teacher education, particularly if these professionals are going to end up in cross-cultural practice. Although the ideal is for affective education to permeate the social work curriculum, an interdisciplinary course entitled "Resolving Intercultural Conflicts" is offered by the author which utilizes simulation games and experimental exercises, and is designed to attain these affective goals (Montalvo, 1983, see Chapter 19).

Chapter 13

TEACHING FOR AFFECTIVE RESPONSES IN PHYSICAL EDUCATION

Craig A. Buschner

Physical education programs are often neglected in school systems, nationwide. Many administrators, parents, and teachers simply do not understand the value and contribution of QUALITY physical education for elementary and secondary students. Unfortunately, there are too many school physical education programs that are not what they should be or can be (Dodds & Locke, 1984; Siedentop, 1980). In addition, recent national studies on schooling overlooked this subject area or implied that physical education was little more than a "curricular frill" (National Commission on Excellence in Education, 1983).

A quality program includes the teaching of motor skills, knowledge, physical fitness, and positive values about activity and exercise. From all the evidence, it appears these values must be learned early and should be reinforced periodically so as to have a continuing influence into adulthood. I contend that if a student is not physically educated during the formative years, he/she may never be. This section addresses goals, motor learning and hemisphericity, holistic teaching, and strategies for obtaining affective results in physical education.

Goals of Physical Education. Most physical educators would agree that the ultimate aim of school physical education is to promote lifetime participation in vigorous physical activities such as exercise, sports, games, dance, gymnastics, aquatics, and outdoor adventure activities. However, deciding upon the goals to reach this aim has been a controversial issue for the past century. The division generally focuses on the priority of *psychomotor* goals (skillful movement and physical fitness), *cognitive* goals (student knowledge), and *affective goals* (feelings, attitudes, interests, values, and social behaviors).

Physical educators have traditionally concentrated on the psychomotor goal as the single, most important and unique contribution to the total education of students. Furthermore, division exists when trying to prioritize skillful movement and physical fitness. Recent societal interest in health and fitness have recently shifted the focus of attention on the poor outcomes of physical fitness test scores of children and youth (U.S. Department of Health and Human Services, 1985). Advocates of the health/fitness curriculum models minimize the necessity for skillful movement and plan experiences that contribute to healthy lifestyles and knowledge about the connection between exercise and wellness. Nevertheless, conflict persists when trying to obtain both goals in a physical education program.

Most physical educators agree that psychomotor goals, especially physical fitness, are easily measured with the availability of valid and reliable tools in the field. Moreover, because of the trend toward educational accountability, physical educators are developing program goals that are easily quantifiable. This trend has decreased the thought of achieving affective goals in physical education. Unfortunately, some physical educators, including Mood (1982), have explicitly warned about the dangers of claiming affective learnings in physical education.

On the other hand, some physical educators (Carlson, 1981; Dodds, 1976; Frye, 1983; Hellison, 1973, 1978, 1985; Marsh, 1984; Mcgee, 1982; Stoner, 1982; Wiese, 1982) take the position that motor skill and physical fitness can both be achieved if the affective domain is activated. Affective behavior might include becoming interested in soccer, wanting to participate in aerobic dance, adhering to a physical fitness program, or maintaining a value to play vigorously and exercise on a daily basis. Siedentop (1980) contends that the central role of the physical educator is to help people learn how to play and to value physical activity. This includes becoming motorically competent, mastering the subject matter, and increasing one's tendencies to engage in physical activity. Similarly, Bain (1980) argues that the goal of physical education is "to socialize the student into the role of participant, to provide the opportunity to learn skills, strategy, customs, and folklore surrounding specific movement activities which he/she finds enjoyable" (p. 48).

While the goals controversy continues, many teachers assume that positive and relevant affective behaviors routinely result from daily learning experiences in physical education class. However, this is an erroneous assumption. Many investigators (Griffin, 1983; Kollen, 1983; Templin, 1981; Tousignant & Siedentop, 1983; Wilson, 1969) have found negative effects of physical education classes on students.

If we are to instill a lifetime of participation in vigorous activity, the primary goal must certainly require both motor skill and knowledge. However, these goals are impractical unless the student values play and exercise. This means that affective goals are to be included. If student affect is important — and it is — the question to address is how to include all three goals in each lesson. Cognitive achievement and psychomotor development should produce affective responses.

Motor Learning and Hemisphericity. The myth that mind and body are separate entities has long been dispelled. Although some perpetuate this unfounded belief, motor learning researchers (Kerr, 1982; Magill, 1985; Oxendine, 1984; Sage, 1984; Stelmach, 1978) have clearly confirmed that people control all of their voluntary physical movements with their minds and not their bodies. Muscular movement is an expression of what is learned and retained by the brain (Kerr, 1982).

Along the same line, hemispheric dominance has received increasing attention in the motor learning literature (Keogh & Sugden, 1985; Sage, 1984: Spirduso, 1978). Some argue that muscular movement is a function of right brain activity (the seat of visual-spatial mentation in most people) because of the spatial relationships required to move efficiently. In fact, some elementary physical educators advocate the movement education model or framework for beginning movers. This paradigm highlights spatial awareness (self and general space) as a prerequisite movement concept for all learning in the psychomotor domain.

The taxonomies of the psychomotor domain (Harrow, 1972; Simpson, 1966) have designated the highest level of learning to encompass

Non-Discursive Communication, Adaptation, and Origination. These concepts parallel the notion of creativity and artistry in movement response. The creation of a modern dance, a new game, an innovative gymnastics routine, or original dunk shot in basketball is an expression of the individual's movement repertoire or movement interpretation. Are these movement examples a function of the right or left cerebral hemisphere? Probably not exclusively from one or the other hemisphere, but an orchestrated effort from both hemispheres.

For example, an efficient motor response requires a person to analyze the intended movements, logically anticipate which movement to use for the situation, and commit the movement to memory so that it can be repeated when needed. In other words, constructing movement routines, identifying rules, and applying strategies may require use of the left (analytical for most people) cerebral hemisphere. When a child is learning to strike a ball with a bat, he/she must cognitively break down the whole movement into parts (analyze) and subsequently put the parts together to form the whole movement or swing. This requires a step-by-step or logical understanding of the movement. Then the movement must be replicated at the appropriate time (as the ball arrives).

Looking more closely at the components of this example, for the child to swing the bat correctly, it is *essential* that there be a motor plan or visual picture of the correct movement to be imitated, especially if the child is trying the striking pattern for the first time. Simpson (1966) classifies this level of learning as the *guided response* stage. This stage includes a movement response or attempt following a model or some criteria against which he/she can compare performance. A performer's attempts to learn a movement will most likely involve imitation and trial and error responses before learning or mastering the skill. Again, it seems as if both cerebral hemispheres must work together so that efficient movement results.

Holistic Teaching. In that students begin physical education classes with different abilities, attitudes, knowledges, motor skills, physical fitness, and styles of learning, it is imperative that teachers plan lessons from a holistic perspective. Objectives should be constructed on the basis that students who participate in movement activities think and move, and subsequently the thought and action positively affect their feelings (Mackenzie, 1969).

Lessons must be so geared as to produce student success. For this to occur, teachers must use a variety of strategies for learning.

The teacher's demonstration techniques are central to the learning of motor skills and the acquisition of positive values. I have found few children, in physical education, who are able to move efficiently without teacher (coach or parent) intervention. A teacher can understand and even verbalize the important concepts of a particular movement. However, my experience is that students need a visual model, picture, film, or positive teacher demonstration of the intended movement. Further, my experience is that some individuals may need a number of demonstrations. For example, it is nearly impossible to perform a flank vault in gymnastics if one fails to visualize what it looks like. A teacher could describe or outline the mechanics of the movement both eloquently and systematically. However, students intuitively know they can learn faster by asking two simple words: "show me."

If the teacher can accurately demonstrate or provide teaching aids and visual stimuli, verbal cues, constructive feedback, and reinforcement the efficient movement patterns and positive attitudes about physical education can result. Teachers of movement must be capable of demonstrating movement patterns for others to learn. Rink (1985) provides five useful guidelines for teacher demonstrations:

1. Demonstrations must be accurate and emphasize only the essential information about the skill.

2. Teachers must share why a skill is performed in a certain way.

3. Teachers must demonstrate the proper organizational format and context of the skill learning.

4. Teachers should have students demonstrate when possible.

5. Teachers should check student understanding following the demonstration by asking questions and then observing.

Obtaining Affective Results. Carlson (1981) said that one of the fundamental techniques for teachers, when working toward affective learning, is to probe students' feelings. Information can be collected through writing samples, class discussion, drawing activities, and Likert scale surveys. For example, responses could be sought in the area of body awareness, physical growth, physical appearance, spatial awareness, effort qualities, sports, games, dance, gymnastics, and exercise.

Griffin (1982) expressed the importance of understanding that both positive and negative experiences can occur on a daily basis in school physical education classes. Positive experiences are, of course, at the heart of affective learning in physical education. Negative experiences, including a negative gymnasium climate, typically result from mindless planning, teaching, and managerial techniques. When students perform motor skills, this becomes public information. When a child takes his/her turn at bat, everyone has an opportunity to judge his/her abilities. The skillful teacher projects these judgements in a positive light for beginners.

There are pitfalls to avoid. Some students develop negative feelings when peers are allowed to choose teams. This is because most students know each other's motor skill level. And, when teams are chosen in public, the last people picked are visibly singled out as the worst players. Also, many teachers continue to test students for physical fitness in front of their classmates. If a student's poor math grade is considered private, then so should one's percentage of body fat. A body comparison test, taken with skinfold calipers, should be measured behind a partition and void of peer knowledge. Furthermore, arguing with teammates and umpires, disputing rules, inability to handle winning and losing, and using profanity, just scratch the surface of negative behaviors that too often occur in physical education classes.

Nevertheless, lack of awareness and managerial strategies to address the above behaviors can have a devastating affect on cognitive and psychomotor learning, and consequently attitude – the affect. Griffin (1982) offers three techniques to measure learning and to increase the teacher's awareness of affective student results:

1. Ask students what they think and how they feel about physical education.

2. Learn to recognize student behavioral cues as indicators of what they think and feel.

3. Reflect on your own instructional and organizational practices in class, especially with regard to avoiding negative experiences.

Implications. Physical education researchers in motor learning and pedagogy are yet to address the issue of hemisphericity and its relationship to student affect when learning motor skills. However, it can be assumed that both hemispheres are integrated during psychomotor learning. Hopefully, future hemispheric research will uncover better ways to learn motor skills.

Meanwhile physical educators need to be concerned with affective results in physical education. Teachers must plan for positive affective responses. Teachers must become aware and sensitive to teaching both hemispheres simultaneously. Teachers must demonstrate and explain. Teaching strategies could include modification of class groupings, selection of certain content, and altering instructional strategies to produce a positive affective state. With concerted effort teachers will understand student interests, attitudes, feelings, beliefs, and values about physical education. Ultimately, teachers will begin to successfully plan and implement lessons that result in students who thoroughly enjoy play and exercise.

CHAPTER 14

QUALITY LEARNING:
A KEY TO MILITARY TRAINING

David L. Sonnier

The United States Army has the highest concern for the training of its personnel. The emphasis is always on preparing to defend the country, even during peacetime. Being prepared can only be accomplished through extensive training and education. This includes both collective and individual training. Collective training includes those activities in which the unit is trained to work as a team to accomplish its wartime mission, often under simulated wartime conditions. But, before the unit can function as a team, the members must each know their own subordinate tasks.

Thus, many hours are spent on individual training. Military training of the individual is done effectively through instructional strategies that employ all three domains of educational pedagogy: the cognitive, the affective, and the psychomotor domains. While individual training is an integral part of collective training, relying heavily on the psychomotor domain, it goes beyond that. Many hours are spent on cognitive development in classroom environments, similar to that of primary, secondary and higher education. Through the years of practice, trial and error, and much research, the Army has developed effectiveness in a strategy that is simple, straightforward, and insures positive results. Competency-based, performance-oriented education includes well-established strategies that are geared for the learning of "hands-on" and experiential tasks. However, the strategy is equally effective in the classroom environment where desired cognitive results can be immediately tested, either orally or with paper and pencil.

Although the strategy is commonly practiced elsewhere, the military classroom differs in that the individuals rarely attend these classes by personal choice. Military instructors have long been faced with a difficult challenge: the individual's presence may be commanded, but this attention cannot be forced. Therefore, instruction must always include strategies that elicit affective results. The lesson must be presented in a manner that not only attracts the learner's attention, but maintains personal involvement throughout the learning process. After all, a bored and inattentive learner reduces the instructor's effectiveness.

Largely because of this, military instructors have long recognized the need to foster affective education. A number of strategies have been found to yield affective results. The learner is rewarded with some form of recognition for individual achievement as often as possible: the list of that day's achievers is posted; those who achieve the task early are allowed a longer water, coffee, or recouperation break; and there is always the awarding of certificates for achievement. The learner's affective attainment is recognized to be as important a factor as his cognitive and psychomotor achievement.

In the military, individual learning can extend from processing enemy intelligence, a cognitive task, to operating mechanical equipment, a psychomotor task. The instructors are normally officers and noncommissioned officers (NCOs), rarely certified to teach in the public schools. In many cases the NCOs have had little or no college education. However, as military educators, they commonly function with effectiveness comparable to professional educators (for further information on military education, see Whittrock, 1986).

A competency-based, performance-oriented task includes first stating the training objective—what is to be accomplished during the particular session. Any training objective will include the following three components:

1. The task that the learners will be able to perform upon completion of the session.

2. The condition(s) under which they will be able to perform the task, for example, given a calculator, a weapon or any other object.

3. The standard(s), or how well the learners are expected to perform the task, often including a time limit.

By constructing the objectives in the form of *task, condition and standard*, the instructor simplifies the difficulty of providing a quality learning experience for the students. The lesson plan includes a list of as many visual aids as are needed to get each point across. By so doing, the preparation is for holistic involvement—both the visual and the linear-logical/analytical propensities are simultaneously involved. The holistic involvement not only prompts a higher degree of cognitive achievement, it also begets affective results. Equally important is the fact that the simple format of this strategy leaves no doubt in the minds of the soldiers about what they are expected to learn. Based on my own observations, there is a general and constant presence of positive affective involvement contributing to this quality of learning.

While the recommended lesson plan has three components, the teaching or delivery is to be conducted in three phases: *introduction, application, and evaluation*. In Phase I, the instructor introduces the training objectives, briefly explains the significance of the task, and provides a demonstration. In phase II, the soldiers practice performing the task, whether it be solving mathematics-related problems or disassembling and assembling a weapon. As much time as necessary to meet the standards is provided. In Phase III, the level of learning is evaluated to insure that all can perform the task within the provided conditions and to the required standards. Those who can are finished, while those who cannot must return to Phase II for more practice. This aspect of the strategy is called a remedial loop.

Because of the high standard of proficiency expectations, this may be one of the areas in which military education may differ from education elsewhere. Educators are generally aware that competency-based, performance-oriented education with a high proficiency expectation cannot normally be planned using a rigid time schedule. Some flexibility must be allowed because different individuals need different amounts of time in order to meet the desired achievement goal.

Military educators also strive to meet the high expectation goal of educating everyone. Additionally, everyone is educated to the fullest extent in the task that is required to be performed. It is affectively oriented in that the learner is more often than not involved and attentive. It is to the holistic nature of the educational strategy that the affective involvement is attributable. As with the educational needs elsewhere, one can never know too much. With competency-based, performance-oriented objectives, *coupled with holistic teaching strategies*, the Army provides an excellent quality of learning for its members. The result is an improved state of preparedness to defend the country.

PART V

EVALUATING HOLISTIC
AND AFFECTIVE EDUCATION

Rex Leonard, Editor

There is a tradition of avoiding measurement and accountance in the management of affective instruction. Indeed, there is a tradition of avoiding affective instruction, entirely. That need not be the case. Evidence is offered lending credence to individual differences due to hemisphericity (CHAPTER 15). Holistic education is a strategy generated by the teacher, the results of which are measured in student success. Student success, teacher accountability, and the supervision of instructional management are confluently described as neuroeducation (CHAPTER 16). Quantity and quality education are given definitive categories (CHAPTER 17), and holistic teaching is empirically evaluated in a definitive study (CHAPTER 18).

R. L.

CHAPTER 15

INDIVIDUAL DIFFERENCES
DUE TO HEMISPHERICITY

Rex Leonard, Patty M. Ward and Douglas W. Schipull

As a result of continuing effort to identify individual differences (Leonard & Boulter, 1985) and the problems that are found in the literature, indications are that in the past analytical learners have been equated with being auditory learners (see misconceptions in Chapter 2). In the development of this instrument, it was necessary to guard against this assumption among other misconceptions. The instrument in its present form is yet in the process of further refinement. However, results are being reported to avoid further delay of the culmination of this project. This chapter is an effort to share the results thus far uncovered, as we continue in our pursuit of identifying the parameters of individual differences that are functions of the hemispheric phenomenon.

It is important to continue studying and identifying the complex of these parameters of individual differences. Educators are especially sensitive to individual differences but have not always known how to deal with the phenomenon. The knowledge of individual differences, as a function of hemispheric preference, is necessary and helpful in order to avoid psychological violations against those who can learn, but who do not grasp immediately because a presentation is geared to the recessive hemisphere. For example, visual learners may not immediately grasp a new concept if a presentation is made verbally, and without visual aids. Further they are not equipped for searching on their own because reading is a chore. Consequently, for a significant number of these students, possibly a fourth or even a third, school can be a place of hurt and embarrassment.

Analytical students could also fall prey to the same feelings. A presentation of visual aids, without sufficient elaboration, could leave these students grasping and frustrated. However, the significant hurt for these students comes from the teaching of misinformation and their attempt to "correct" the teacher. They fall prey to wrath. Thus, hemispheric preference has a wealth of information for educators. However, its greatest impact is on how to maintain a positive affective environment by reaching and teaching all students (see *Holistic Education*, Chapter 3).

Leonard and Boulter (1985) made some preliminary gains on the establishment of an instrument to measure the modes of consciousness in humans. In the interim, many of the suggestions were incorporated in the improvement of this instrument. In the process, it became increasingly clear that even the most subtle among the parameters of individual differences could very well be hemisphericity based. These discussions describe the continuing development of a simple checklist instrument to obtain these data.

The evidence sought concerned individual differences and if they have parallel relations with the fact that one's cerebral hemisphere processes linear-logical data in a sequential manner, often associated with the left hemisphere in most people. The other hemisphere processes visual, configurational data in a holistic manner, often associated with the right hemisphere in most people. It appeared plausible to assume that these are the basic propensities for thought processing and that each in pure form, should be found in a few individuals at either side of a near-normal curve distribution. It was expected that the vast majority of persons in the distribution should orchestrate the two propensities in a blended manner. However, even in the majority of these individuals, a preferred mode was expected. Also it was expected that a small population, the number being of approximately the same as the two extreme populations, should rest squarely centered—utilizing both propensities in a nonpreferential manner.

With these basic assumptions, the instrument was revised and administered to a number of college groups with a high degree of randomness among them between 1985 and 1987. In its evolution, the instrument was applied in large (over 60 students) to medium (approximately 30 students) college classes. A relatively representative sample could be obtained from students that were enrolled in Fundamentals of Science courses, specifically Fundamentals of Physical Science. This is a required course for all students, including many computer science students, as well as science majors who are enrolled in Teacher Education programs. Therefore, these students represent not completely, but perhaps satisfactorily a sample of all students attending the university.

Development of this instrument included specific items from three parameters, assumed to be hemisphericity based: thinking styles, learning styles, and social styles. While there is yet more work to be done to bring this simple instrument to its final form, we feel that the present status can be reported for the purpose of soliciting further research in such an easy-to-administer assessment of individual differences due to hemispheric preference (The items are listed with the tables of data).

The design of the investigation at this point included the following questions:

1. Is there an indication of small populations at either extreme of the normal curve distribution with highly visual and highly analytical propensities?

2. Is there an indication of a population at the middle of the normal curve population showing orchestrated utility of both, but with a preference for neither of the two propensities?

A Likert type scale was developed to show strength of dominance between the two sides of the brain. Codes indicating frequency of activity on the Likert scale were as follows: 1) Never, 2) Occasionally, 3) Frequently, and 4) Always. The memory evaluation items, 7 and 20, were exceptions as they were coded: 1) Not Good, 2) Fair, 3) Good, and 4) Very Accurate. In order to validate the present instrument, a sample of 51 undergraduate students was used for a pre- and post-administration. Table 1 presents results of the items that were developed along with the percentage distribution for each item on both pre- and post-test. Generally, most items had distributions that were similar on the pre- and post-tests, indicating stability over time. Furthermore, the data displayed in Table 15.1 suggest affirmative answers to the design questions.

TABLE 15.1 QUESTIONNAIRE

Percent of Responses on Questionnaire

		1	2	3	4
1. I form a mental picture of my thoughts.	PRE		37	58	5
	POST		30	61	9
2. My new ideas result from systematic reasoning.	PRE	2	38	57	3
	POST	2	37	61	
3. I reach conclusions based on intuition.	PRE		48	49	3
	POST		46	50	4
4. I remember dates well.	PRE	7	40	37	17
	POST	6	33	50	11
5. I sequence my thoughts exclusively using logic & reason	PRE		33	60	7
	POST	2	39	48	11
6. My memory is most efficient when I recall a mental picture of an event.	PRE		15	40	45
	POST		13	48	39
7. My memory, with regard to specific events, is:	PRE	2	18	52	28
	POST		23	58	19
8. I tend to formulate my ideas through a process of thinking about & organizing known facts.	PRE		22	67	12
	POST	2	26	65	7
9. I tend to find solutions to problems by visualizing the whole picture within my mind.	PRE		30	57	13
	POST		24	61	15
10. My memory is efficient when I can recall a sequence of events in time without a visual cue.	PRE	7	67	22	5
	POST	7	67	22	4
11. My ideas originate with sudden insight.	PRE	2	55	42	2
	POST	2	54	43	2
12. When I am inclined to do something I tend to consult with other people & gather as much research evidence as I can about the activity before proceeding.	PRE	3	40	42	15
	POST	2	56	37	6
13. When I am learning, I like visual aids to be used.	PRE		17	42	42
	POST		15	50	35
14. When I observe significant events in real life or in the media, such as sports tournaments or musical performances, I tend to cheer or applaud.	PRE	2	23	50	25
	POST	2	32	41	26
15. I assimilate information from reading material when it is presented in a sequential manner & without pictorial rhetoric.	PRE		64	32	3
	POST	4	57	37	2
16. I learn through listening to an explanation.	PRE		22	67	12
	POST		30	56	15

			1	2	3	4
17.	In my work & recreational activities I would rather be closely involved with people.	PRE	2	15	47	37
		POST	2	17	50	32
18.	When reading to learn, I like the author to paint a vivid picture with words.	PRE		7	38	55
		POST		9	48	43
19.	I tend to formulate new ideas through a process of visualizing, & building the whole story with various components.	PRE		30	57	13
		POST		28	67	6
20.	My memory, with regard to specific dates in time, is:	PRE	8	38	40	13
		POST	7	41	43	9
21.	In my recreational activities, I would rather drive vehicles or use athletic equipment.	PRE	12	43	35	10
		POST	7	50	32	11
22.	I consider information logically & reach conclusions through an orderly process.	PRE	2	28	65	5
		POST		32	63	6
23.	When making a decision I rely on the opinions of other people in real life &/or the media.	PRE	7	57	35	2
		POST	4	67	30	
24.	Specific things that happened in the past tend to escape my memory.	PRE	17	70	10	3
		POST	17	74	9	
25.	I solve problems by sequencing the facts in logical order.	PRE		35	60	5
		POST		39	56	6
26.	I look upon sports or other significant events analytically & do not show outward emotion.	PRE	37	52	12	
		POST	30	59	11	
27.	I prefer to consider facts, either observed or read, when making decisions.	PRE		23	63	13
		POST		26	63	11
28.	When inclined to do something I tend to begin promptly–based on my own decisions without consultation from others.	PRE	13	45	37	5
		POST	4	63	32	2

1 = Never, 2 = Occasionally, 3 = Frequently, 4 = Always
Exceptions: 7, 20 1 = Not Good, 2 = Fair, 3 = Good, 4 = Very Accurate

The results in Table 15.1 are further substantiated by the findings displayed in Table 15.2. The means and standard deviations by items support the consistency of responses from pre- to post-test in that the average response changed very little, moreover, the standard deviation across each item on pre- and post-test were quite consistent, indicating that the level of agreement about the item responses remained about the same across all the items.

TABLE 15.2 MEANS & STANDARD DEVIATIONS

ITEM (ABBREVIATED)	MEANS		STD DEV	
	Pre	Post	Pre	Post
1. Mental Picture of Thoughts	2.7	2.8	.6	.6
2. Systematic Reasoning	2.6	2.6	.6	.5
3. Intuitive Conclusions	2.6	2.6	.6	.6
4. Remember Dates Well	2.6	2.7	.8	.8
5. Sequence Thoughts Through Reason	2.7	2.7	.6	.7
6. Mental Picture of Events	3.3	3.3	.7	.7
7. Memory of Specific Events	3.1	3.0	.7	.6
8. Ideas Through Known Facts	2.9	2.8	.6	.6
9. Solutions by Visualizing Whole	2.8	2.9	.6	.6
10. Memory Based on Sequence Without Visual	2.2	2.2	.6	.6
11. Origination of Ideas Through Sudden Insight	2.4	2.4	.6	.6
12. Decisions Based on Active Research	2.7	2.5	.8	.6
13. Learn With Visual Aids	3.2	3.2	.7	.7
14. Enthusiastic Observer	3.0	2.9	.7	.8
15. Assimilate Info Without Visual Reference	2.4	2.4	.6	.6
16. Learn Through Listening	2.9	2.8	.6	.7
17. Like to Work With People	3.2	3.1	.7	.7
18. Read With Pictorial Portrayal	3.5	3.3	.6	.6
19. New Ideas Through Visualizing Whole	2.8	2.8	.6	.5
20. Memory of Dates and Times	2.6	2.5	.8	.8
21. Leisure Use of Vehicles or Athletic Equipment	2.4	2.5	.8	.8
22. Conclusions Through Orderly Process	2.7	2.7	.6	.6
23. Decisions Through Others or Media	2.3	2.3	.6	.5
24. Past Events Escape Memory	2.0	1.9	.6	.5
25. Solutions By Sequencing Facts Logically	2.7	2.7	.6	.6
26. Events and Sports Without Emotion	1.8	1.8	.6	.6
27. Decisions Through Facts Observed or Read	2.9	2.8	.6	.6
28. Decisions Promptly Through Self	2.3	2.3	.8	.6

Image factor analysis of the instrument was performed in order to establish construct validity and to furnish further evidence of stability by using correlations. Initial factorization of all items using Kaiser's rule showed five factors with Eigenvalues greater than or equal to one. However, examination of the Eigenvalues revealed a break in the pattern after the third factor. Thus three factors were used in the final analysis, results of which are shown in Table 15.3.Further evidence of stability beyond that provided in Tables 15.1, and 15.2,was obtained by the factorization of the pre- as well as the post-test.The results in Table 15.3 indicate only minor changes in the factor loadings from pre- to post-test.

TABLE 15.3 FACTOR ANALYSIS ROTATED LOADINGS

	PRETEST FACTORS			POSTTEST FACTORS		
	1	2	3	1	2	3
1. Mental Picture of Thoughts	-02	22	51	30	13	46
2. Systematic Reasoning	-42	30	24	57	-38	-03
3. Intuitive Conclusions	20	-24	10	28	12	17
4. Remember Dates Well	79	-01	-13	04	82	-26
5. Sequence Thoughts Through Reason	03	69	-11	80	-05	09
6. Mental Picture of Events	06	00	58	18	-01	81
7. Memory of Specific Events	68	-02	14	21	83	11
8. Ideas Through Known Facts	12	68	24	68	06	17
9. Solutions by Visualizing Whole	-01	12	58	31	18	63
10. Memory Based on Sequence Without Visual	07	24	-16	01	03	-23
11. Origination of Ideas Through Sudden Insight	31	-25	29	06	-20	-06
12. Decisions Based on Active Research	-06	24	39	49	-03	44
13. Learn With Visual Aids	-25	-05	53	-04	15	70
14. Enthusiastic Observer	39	17	09	33	38	28
15. Assimilate Info Without Visual Reference	06	35	-13	25	06	07
16. Learn Through Listening	18	24	19	-15	33	18
17. Like to Work With People	42	16	12	17	36	13
18. Read With Pictorial Portrayal	04	-15	45	-09	09	60
19. New Ideas Through Visualizing Whole	11	-04	53	34	13	54
20. Memory of Dates and Time	74	11	-21	17	76	-23
21. Leisure Use of Vehicles or Athletic Equipment	12	13	02	40	16	05
22. Conclusions Through Orderly Process	-02	72	13	84	-09	-05
23. Decisions Through Others or Media	-08	-02	15	18	-01	26
24. Past Events Escape Memory	-70	-17	19	03	-56	-05
25. Solutions By Sequencing Facts Logically	11	65	07	75	-10	10
26. Events and Sports Without Emotion	-43	-09	11	-22	-32	-03
27. Decisions Through Facts Observed or Read	-16	42	-01	59	16	04
28. Decisions Promptly Through Self	01	15	05	01	-16	-04
EIGENVALUES	3.4	2.9	2.0	5.1	3.0	2.4

Factor 1 and 2 on the pre-test, however, did change positions in importance on the post-test. Factor 1 appears to be dominated by memory evaluation items (Items 4, 7, 20, and 24). A dimension consisting of attributes having to do with logical, sequential, and orderly mental processing of information (Items 2, 5, 8, 22, and 25) was the principal construct in factor 2. Factor 3 portrays a dimension having to do with elements of visualization linked to learning and processing information (Items 1, 6, 9, 13, 18, and 19).

Additional evidence of stability-type reliability is contained in Table 15.4. Pre- and post-test correlations for each of the items show reliability coefficients ranging from 0 to .67 with most items having a moderate value. In addition, the items pertaining to visual reference were pooled and showed a test/retest reliability of .64 across the 14 visually referenced items. The remaining 14 items were pooled and showed a test/retest reliability coefficient of .62 for the analytic items.

Cronbach Alpha coefficients were computed on the total test as well as visual and analytical items. These coefficients were also run for pre- and post-test on each of the foregoing. Internal consistency for all items on the pre-test was .64 which increased slightly to .67 when computed on the post-test. The visual items as noted in Table 15.4 produced an alpha coefficient of .54 on the pre-test which also increased to .64 for the post-test. The analytic items produced an alpha coefficient of .60 on the pre-test and increased slightly for a .67 on the post-test.

In summary, this instrument appears to strike a medium between an instrument having more items which would offer gains in reliability versus the disadvantage of having an instrument with too few items.

The instrument demonstrated, in this sample of 51 students, substantial stability over time. Most items showed moderate stability coefficients when examined individually. Test/retest reliability coefficients and internal consistency alpha measures all exceeded .5 when scoring scales consisting of visual and analytic items were tested. Moreover, image factorization of the test showed stability of the factors over time. Thus, not only were means, standard deviations, and percentage response distributions stable in the sample across time, but also correlations showed consistency both in magnitude

TABLE 15.4 RELIABILITIES

	CORRELATION	VARIABLES PRE/POST
* 1.	Mental Picture of Thoughts	65
2.	Systematic Reasoning	32
* 3.	Intuitive Conclusions	47
4.	Remember Dates Well	75
5.	Sequence Thoughts Through Reason	30
* 6.	Mental Picture of Evente	51
7.	Memory of Specific Events	57
8.	Ideas Through Known Facts	36
* 9.	Solutions by Visualizing Whole	57
10.	Memory Based on Sequence Without Visual	23
* 11.	Origination of Ideas Through Sudden Insight	22
12.	Decisions Based on Active Research	55
* 13.	Learn With Visual Aids	61
* 14.	Enthusiastic Observer	59
15.	Assimilate Info Without Visual Reference	00
16.	Learn Through Listening	50
* 17.	Like to Work With People	75
* 18.	Read With Pictorial Portrayal	55
* 19.	New Ideas Through Visualizing Whole	39
* 20.	Memory of Dates and Times	68
21.	Leisure Use of Vehicles/Athletic Equipment	67
22.	Conclusions Through Orderly Process	25
* 23.	Decisions Through Others or Media	39
* 24.	Past Events Escape Memory	41
25.	Solutions By Sequencing Facts Logically	41
26.	Events and Sports Without Emotion	64
27.	Decisions Through Facts Observed or Read	44
* 28.	Decisions Promptly Through Self	17

* Items pertaining to visual reference 64
  Items pertaining to analytical brain functioning (remaining items) 62

and direction across time. The instrument has technically improved substantially since the last project (Leonard & Boulter, 1985). The authors suggest that the instrument needs further study to evaluate norms as well as to refine validity and reliability.

CHAPTER 16

HEMISPHERICITY BASED INSTRUCTIONAL MANAGEMENT AND ACCOUNTABILITY: SUPERVISING DELIVERY

Elaine F. Fish

Hemispheric preference is one of the basic elements for consideration in instructional management. Because some individuals are visually oriented and others are analytically oriented, differences in students' learning styles emerge. Teachers are likewise different because of hemispheric preference. Visually oriented teachers tend to be student-centered and use the *self-directed* mode of teaching. Analytically oriented teachers tend to be subject-centered and have more success using the *authoritarian mode*. Although the vast majority of teachers are *eclectic* and blend the two modes, it is from the two extremes, extremely visual and extremely analytical, that one gets to know and understand these differences created by hemispheric preference (teaching modes and philosophies are more adequately discussed in Part I).

Hemisphericity has special implications on both instructional management and the supervisory activities that are used to determine accountability. *Hemisphericity based instructional management* (HBIM) deals with the personal matter of teaching mode preferences. While HBIM should be considered a highly individualized and personal activity, *hemisphericity based accountability* (HBA) has universal application with a common set of competence expectancy across teaching modes and philosophies because it deals with teaching results and outcomes. Confluently, HIBM and HBA can be called *neuroeducation*.

Neuroeducation requires extensive use of visual aids in instruction, as defined in holistic education. It also means that when teaching a subject, the teacher should never assume that students already know something, or that to include a more elementary or minute detail would be redundant or insulting to their intelligence, thus excluding information or an example which might greatly enhance clarity. On the contrary, the subject should be explained in a concise step-by-step manner, until each visual aid has been thoroughly explained. Conversely, when describing a phenomenon, visual aids MUST accompany every aspect of these explanations, blending oral presentation with visual aids that result in a lesson that is appropriate for the varying learning styles within the class. Neuroeducation also requires adequate setting, facilities, and lessons that are planned and presented at an appropriate degree of difficulty with the students' achievement, ability and level of maturity in mind.

To Whom is the Teacher Accountable? In that HBIM is more adequately discussed elsewhere as *holistic education*, HBA is not elsewhere discussed and is the subject of this chapter. HBA should be a continuous process in a teacher's self-evaluation routine. A teacher is first of all accountable for the achievement of personal gratification for a job well done. Next, a teacher is accountable to the students. After all, the students are directly the consumers of the product we dispense—we teach and they learn. Finally, the teacher is accountable to the parents and to the community served by the school. The supervisory personnel represent the rights and interests of the community in holding each teacher accountable for acceptable levels of competence and performance.

Holding the Learner Accountable. Maintaining accountability among the students means documenting that they are engaged in the learning process and motivated to learn. The supervisor, principal, or coordinator is a third party to the process, with parental and community interest, and should be able to observe students involved in their own growth process. Student involvement is student involvement, no matter how it was generated. Thus, it is not the supervisor's task to determine if the teacher is student-centered or subject-centered, self-directed or authoritarian, but rather to observe the degree to which students are actively engaged, with the appropriate materials, and with a high success rate in the learning process.

Holding the Teacher Accountable. Teacher accountability is an ongoing process, best performed introspectively. Student achievement measures the best data for any valid introspective interpretation of successful teaching. Before the advent of any supervisory activity, the third party to the learning process, a teacher should have an ongoing way of determining the degree of success being achieved and maintained. That success is typically measured from the cognitive achievement level (the quantity learned) with relation to the level of affective involvement of the students (the quality of learning).

Teachers should have an awareness of their own preferred mode of teaching: if visually oriented, success is more than likely to come from a self-directed, student-centered environment. The analytical teacher is prone to be successful if the authoritarian environment is maintained. *It is not up to a supervisor to make this determination.* The supervisor's task is to assist the teacher in enhancing quantity learned and the quality of the results.

The supervisor has a right to demand that holistic strategies be employed, that the visual aids include a bulletin board on the topic being taught, that students be actively involved in the learning process, and that they display a reasonable degree of positive affect. Any display of negative affect is not only a violation of the students' rights, but is a violation of the rights and interests of the parents and the community.

Hemisphericity Based Accountability in Supervisory Activities. Supervisors are likewise biased by their own hemispheric nature. A visually oriented person is most likely to place priority and esteem on student-centered activities. The analytical person is more than likely to be impressed with subject-centered activities and may even be critical of student-centeredness. Acknowledgement of this bias is the first step toward avoiding discrimination. And, with that level of understanding should come tolerance.

What then, is the supervisor to look for when evaluating the teaching/learning process? First, teaching and learning are two distinctly different processes, hopefully producing a cause-and-effect relationship, if properly managed. The effectiveness of the *learning process* can be discerned by observing the students. The effectiveness of the *teaching process* can be discerned by observing the teacher's activities. Because it is in the hands of the teacher to generate the learning process for the students, supervision should start with an evaluation of the teacher's managerial skills.

Second, neuroeducation dictates the implementation of holistic educational strategies. Some *specific observations* of teacher-performance to be noted in evaluating success with HBA include:

1. Is the lesson appropriate for the ability level of the group?

2. Are visual aids adequate and appropriate?

3. Are the objectives of the lesson being met?

Third, among the *general observations* that can be made, an important one includes: Does the teacher use some of the activities that are rich and fertile with holistic involvement and promote affective results (see Part VI: Instructional Strategies that Promote Affective Results)? While making these observations, the hemispheric or philosophical persuasion of the teacher *is of no concern* to the supervisor (unless there is a suspicion that the teacher may be more successful practicing in a different mode. If such is the case, and by mutual consent, the teacher may observe a master teacher that employs the appropriate mode). *Student involvement is his/her ONLY concern.*

In conclusion, the teaching/learning/supervisory processes of HBIM and HBA, and neuroeducation in general, hinge on the degree to which the students are engaged in cognitive achievement (the quantity learned), and the affective results that are generated (the quality of the learning) by those processes (see Chapter 17 for success/failure determinations).

QUANTITY AND QUALITY EDUCATION: MEASURING AFFECTIVE LEARNING

Isadore L. Sonnier, Giovanni Fontecchio and Martha G. Dow

Elementary science teachers should become aware that any learning environment invariably permeates with the presence of one of the three affective states, although on an individual basis, the students are collectively experiencing either positive, neutral, or negative affective attainment. While the attainment of positive results is the most commendable level of teacher achievement, neutral results are none-the-less acceptable. However, negative affective results can never be an acceptable level of affective attainment, especially at this, the elementary school level where lasting impressions are so easily learned.

One way to monitor these efforts is to routinely measure the level of both individual and collective affective attainment among the students. Through such measurements, any teacher can accurately determine the quality resulting from his/her teaching efforts. If these teaching efforts tend to elicit neutral or even negative attainment, knowing this can help the teacher to make the necessary adjustment toward professional improvement. A point of confusion that may have hampered affective evaluation in the past could have resulted from the mistaken impression that teaching and learning are one, single, undifferentiated activity, instead of viewing them as two, separate entities. While both result from the efficiency and effectiveness of teaching activities, cognitive achievement best describes the level of student participation in these learning activities. The level of affective attainment best describes the efficiency and effectiveness of the teaching activities. The measurement of affective learning requires the distinguishing QUANTITY = HOW MUCH was learned from QUALITY = HOW WELL a learning experience was developed by the teacher.

Teachers are usually apprehensive about being evaluated by their supervisors. However, it is possible to periodically monitor student progress, and at the same time gain confidence with success in the ongoing teaching/learning processes. Any teacher can monitor both, the amount (quantity) of cognitive achievement with relation to the level of affective attainment (quality of learning) by the students.

Along with the students' cognitive achievement and affective attainment should come self-confidence and personal pride in outstanding and commendable professional achievement. This information is requested and obtained from the students, themselves. They are asked to candidly evaluate the level of their cognitive achievement with respect to the level of affective attainment. The students are, after all, directly the consumers of the educational product we dispense. A checklist is provided to help the teacher to obtain the needed information (see Figure 17.1). Values that are indicated in Question 1 concerning the grade earned (or to be earned) are paired with Question 3, the rate of affective involvement. Note that "a lot" = *positive affect,* "some" = *neutral affect,* and "very little" = *negative affect* (see Sonnier, 1981, 1985).

The student data are to be compiled so as to indicate Question 1, the cognitive achievement and Question 3, affective attainment, as related with the four categories in Figure 17.2 and explanation in Figure 17.3. Category 1 = learned a lot and enjoyed the lesson a lot. Category 2 = learned a lot, but did not enjoy. Category 3 = did not learn a lot, but enjoyed. Category 4 = neigher learned a lot, nor enjoyed. While everyone will agree with Category 1 as the most commendable and Category 4 as the least commendable, teachers will differ in philosophy with Categories 2 and 3. Authoritarian, subject-centered teachers will feel most comfortable with Category 2 and not quite so comfortable with Category 3. However, self-directed, student-centered teachers will feel most comfortable with Category 3 and less so with Category 2. They were placed in this order because of the traditional values, rather than which is right or wrong as can be debat-

A CHECKLIST FOR COGNITIVE
ACHIEVEMENT/AFFECTIVE ATTAINMENT

Lesson _____

1. I made (or expect to make) on the tests and quizzes of this lesson:
   _____A   _____B   _____C   _____D   _____F

2. This grade is: better than _____, equal to _____, or less than _____, the amount I learned.

3. I enjoyed learning this lesson: a lot _____, some _____, very little _____ .

4. The pacing of the lesson was: too fast _____, okay _____, too slow.

5. How could the lesson have been presented to help you learn and enjoy materials more?

Comments: _____

_____

_____

_____

_____

FIGURE 17.1

ed. These assessments are always to be kept candid and anonymous and
the student made aware of this discretion. If more teachers were to turn
to the students for these determinations, and were to use these criticisms
and suggestions as means of improving instruction, our educational system
and the quality of learning would undoubtedly improve.

If a teacher were to present a lesson to the students and the results of
that assessment to be a low score, even though he/she thought it was a
great teaching job, the teacher is made aware of the problem and soon learns
that it can be corrected. If not for the present group, the lesson can be re-
written for the next presentation. Experience is that 80 percent achievement 80 percent of the time of Category 1 is very good. Anything lower
is less than desirable.

In this regard, it is important for the teacher to consider himself/herself
a dispenser of knowledge, much as a salesperson is a dispenser of a product.
The criticism is of the product, not the salesperson. What the students are
telling the teacher, by reacting negatively to a lesson presented, is that

THE FOUR CATEGORIES OF STUDENT EVALUATION

CATEGORY 1

LEARNED A LOT, ENJOYED A LOT

Lesson _____

1. I made (or expect to make) on the tests and quizzes of this lesson:

   XX A   XX B   XX C   D   F

2. This grade is: better than ____, equal to ____, or less than ____, the amount I learned. _____

3. I enjoyed learning this lesson: a lot XX , some XX , very little _____

4. The pacing of the lesson was: too fast _____ , okay _____ , too slow. _____

5. How could the lesson have been presented to help you learn and enjoy materials more?

Comments: _____ In Category 1, students indicate a learning level of
   A, B, or C and mark having enjoyed the lesson
   a lot, or at least some. _____

CATEGORY 2

LEARNED A LOT, ENJOYED SOME OR LITTLE

Lesson _____

1. I made (or expect to make) on the tests and quizzes of this lesson:

   XX A   XX B   XX C   D   F

2. This grade is: better than ____, equal to ____, or less than ____, the amount I learned. _____

3. I enjoyed learning this lesson: a lot _____ some XX , very little XX

4. The pacing of the lesson was: too fast _____ , okay _____ , too slow. _____

5. How could the lesson have been presented to help you learn and enjoy materials more?

Comments: _____ In Category 2, students indicate a learning level of
   A, B, or C and mark having enjoyed the lesson
   very little. _____

CATEGORY 3

LEARNED LITTLE, ENJOYED A LOT

Lesson _____

1. I made (or expect to make) on the tests and quizzes of this lesson:

   A   B   C   XX D   XX F

2. This grade is: better than ____, equal to ____, or less than ____, the amount I learned. _____

3. I enjoyed learning this lesson: a lot XX , some XX , very little _____

4. The pacing of the lesson was: too fast _____ , okay _____ , too slow. _____

5. How could the lesson have been presented to help you learn and enjoy materials more?

Comments: _____ In Category 3, students indicate a learning level of
   D or F but mark having enjoyed the lesson
   a lot, or at least some. _____

CATEGORY 4

LEARNED LITTLE, ENJOYED VERY LITTLE

Lesson _____

1. I made (or expect to make) on the tests and quizzes of this lesson:

   A   B   C   XX D   XX F

2. This grade is: better than ____, equal to ____, or less than ____, the amount I learned. _____

3. I enjoyed learning this lesson: a lot _____ some _____ very little XX

4. The pacing of the lesson was: too fast _____ , okay _____ , too slow. _____

5. How could the lesson have been presented to help you learn and enjoy materials more?

Comments: _____ In Category 4, students indicate a learning level of
   D or F and mark having enjoyed the lesson
   very little. _____

FIGURE 17.2

FOUR CATEGORIES OF COGNITIVE ACHIEVEMENT/AFFECTIVE ATTAINMENT

(A) COGNITIVE ACHIEVEMENT	(B) AFFECTIVE ATTAINMENT
1. STUDENTS LEARNED A LOT	AND ENJOYED THE LESSON A LOT
2. STUDENTS LEARNED A LOT	BUT DID NOT ENJOY THE LESSON
3. STUDENTS DID NOT LEARN MUCH	BUT ENJOYED THE LESSON
4. STUDENTS DID NOT LEARN MUCH	AND DID NOT ENJOY THE LESSON

FIGURE 17.3

The effectiveness of a lesson taught can be determined by comparing the amount of cognitive achievement (the quantity learned) through the usual unit or end-of-lesson test. Affective attainment can be determined by simply asking the students if they DID or DID NOT enjoy learning that lesson. The results provide a way to determine the appropriateness of any lesson plan, and may even provide clues on how to improve its next presentation (After Sonnier, 1981).

the lesson went too fast, too slow (rarely the case), or was inappropriate for the audience. A closer look at the materials, in addition to the students' comments and criticisms, could reveal precisely the way to correct the problem with the proper adjustments for the next presentation.

Further, if the teacher is to be accountable for the materials presented, it is the teacher's responsibility to prepare in advance for different levels of ability, just in case some of the students learn more rapidly than expected, and to have enrichment materials for those who learn at a slower pace. Often the entire group benefits from materials that meet the needs of the fast as well as the slow learner. In either case, the student evaluations will greatly enhance the future preparation and presentation of the same lesson plan.

The final suggestion is that these evaluations come from the students without fear of teacher retribution, retaliation, or punishment of any sort. The teacher should receive the student evaluations as criticisms of the product – not the salesperson. From the student's view, the evaluation is shared honestly, it is often frankly stated, and he/she thinks that it should be appreciated by the teacher.

CHAPTER 18

A STRATEGY FOR EMPIRICALLY EVALUATING HOLISTIC TEACHING

Miguel A. Santos Rego, Lisardo Doval Salgado and Luis M. Sobrado Fernandez

"What could be more beautiful than to have students achieve in a new academic area. It is like learning a second language."

A. de la Garanderie

A number of grade 6, 7, and 8 teachers were instructed in how to implement holistic educational strategies as a part of their inservice program in teacher education on the Galacia campus of the University of Santiago de Compostela (Spain). Among these, six were selected to participate in the present investigation to determine if holistic educational strategies were superior to those traditionally used. Among the six, three of the teachers were selected because they were self-reported as visually oriented (an implied preference for self-directed classroom management) and the other three because they were analytically oriented (an implied preference for authoritarian classroom management). This determination was made as a result of the mode of thinking/learning test (see the updated version, Figure 18.1, p. 140).

The teachers were asked to teach their classes in two ways: 1) as they normally would (Treatment Group A, the control group) and 2) using holistic educational strategies (treatment Group B, the experimental group). For comparison of the results, the simple statistical design B-A was applied so as to obtain positive results if the hypothesis was correct (holistic teaching is superior) or, negative results (the hypothesis was incorrect).

The results obtained from the raw scores of cognitive achievement in the visual teachers' classes were indicated by a range of 0.07 to -.52, the mean favoring holistic teaching was 0.28 (see Table 18.1, page 140). There were a total of eight among the 72 students to indicate affective achievement at the Category 1 level (learned a lot and enjoyed the lesson a lot, see Figure 18.2, page 141).

The results in the analytical teachers' classes were indicated by a range of -0.08 to 0.29 in cognitive achievement with a mean of 0.10 favoring holistic teaching. And, 47 among the 86 students indicated affective achievement at the Category I level.

For both groups, there was a total raw score of 0.18 in cognitive achievement favoring holistic teaching and 55 of the 158 students achieved at the Category I level.

R.L.

It is cruel for the educational community to brand some children failures. For these unfortunate children, we have noted that scholastic activities are characterized with anxiety, frustration, and a general attitude of uselessness. And, in Spain, they represent more than 35 percent of the elementary school population.

Psychologists and sociologists are attempting to find out-of-school causes for this phenomenon. However, it is of no help for teachers who have no control over the problems that students encounter out-of-school. Nonetheless, we are convinced that educators must take full responsibility for neutralizing this problem of excessive scholastic failure. It is our view that children are not born to be failures. On the contrary, it is something that happens to them in the classroom. Although the problem is created in the classroom, few are looking into the classroom for the solution to this problem.

Along those lines, we discuss several categories of individual differences in thinking and learning that may show evidence for rethinking of instructional objectives and teaching methods.

Individual differences and Instructional Methods. Individual differences among learners continues to be a major concern among educators. However, it was not until educators became aware of the cognitive paradigm, that some of us are visually oriented and others of us are anlytically oriented, that they were able to focus on and gain a better understanding of individual differences among learners. For example, a better understanding of cognitive (thinking/learning/social) styles would help explain individual differences among students, as well as different instructor's needs for different instructional objectives. A general definition of cognitive styles is that they are those processes by which personality development unfolds into individual differences, apparently a function basic to hemisphericity.

Instructional objectives are those goals, built with content base, that are so constructed as to maximize the performance of different students. Thus, these objectives should be sufficiently diverse as to meet the collective minds of different individuals. Holistic strategies satisfy the needs of both, visually and analytically oriented learners. Our concern is for the uplifting of all students. Holistic strategies help analytical learners to become more visual and visual learners to become more analytical. It is the latter that benefit the most. Traditionally, teaching methods were not suited to their learning style and has left many of these students with a poor self-esteem, and, a tendency to waste time and effort. For these reasons, some students achieve poorly. Others excel as well as gain a sense of pleasure in learning under the same circumstances.

The Cognitive Styles. A review of the literature reveals a variety of conflicting definitions of cognitive styles. There are those who address themselves to "the principles of cognitive control," and "cognitive strategies"; those who relate cognitive styles as the manifestation of a wide variety of personalities, and, yet others, who speak of cognitive styles exclusively as individual differences, relative to the processes and procedures employed in problem solving. ". . . From the beginning, the study of cognitive styles has hinged upon either a strictly cognitive impression or the impression of different aspects of the personality that are either directly or indirectly related to individual differences" (Carretero and Palacios, 1982a, p. 23).

It may clear the atmosphere to remember the two dimensions of the human personality: the ideologic dimension of past experiences and the dynamic dimension of the present. In effect, they converge into the configuration of habits, talents, and attitudes, and they are the basis for personality and other individual differences. Taking the position that life's events do not take place at random, the potential of one's individual differences are prematurely conditioned by existing circumstances that cause one to acquire habits and cognitive processess, thereby instilling personal strategies that interface with the objective field of knowledge.

Witkin, a prominent researcher on this topic, defined cognitive styles as the "characteristic way of functioning, revealed through each of his/her own way of perceiving as expressed in intellectual activities" (see Messick, 1977, taken from Garcia Ramos, 1982, 612). Kogan (1981, 306) said that "individual differences in perceiving, remembering and thinking are as distinctly different as ways of learning, storing, transferring, and using information."

Two sources of cognitive style studies most discussed in the literature come from tests of perception. They are the "matching of embedded figures" (Kagan, et al., 1964) and the "identification of embedded figures" (Witkin, et al. 1977) which are used as the basis for these tests. The two basic types of cognitive styles which emerged from these tests are the impulsive and reflective personality types. Briefly, the impulsive person shows a tendency toward hastily completing a task, thus making mistakes. The reflective person, on the other hand, confronts a task more carefully and in an analytical manner. Evidence from these tests indicate that the same tendencies exist in children, an implication of their cognitive styles. We will return to this discussion later to point out that other conditions may cause the anxieties relative to being an impulsive person. These tests indicate that the impulsive person is hampered by confusion, tension, and anxiety. These tensions, which have been identified as derived from the fear of failure, prevent positive motivation and any hope for achievement.

The "embedded figure test" of Witkin has lead to the well-known description of two different cognitive styles, field dependence and field independence. Presented with a simple geometric figure embedded in a more complex figure, the subject is to perceive the simple figure. Some discover the hidden figure almost immediately. Others are distracted and waste time even in dealing with the simplest of tasks. The different levels of achievement in these tests are not only interpreted to reflect perceptual talents, but they also are interpreted to indicate the existence of different thinking styles. As a result of the Witkin studies came the distinction of such individual differences in perceiving as the *global style* (field dependent) and the *articulate style* (field independent).

Although there may not be an absolute relation, we suggest a parallel relationship between these cognitive styles and learning strategies: The articulated style corresponds to a "serialist" strategy while the global corresponds to a "holistic" strategy. "When you give students a choice between a series of 'abstract' topics and a parallel series of 'real world' tasks, the serialist type proceeds in a step-by-step manner through the abstract task, as well as with the one taken from a real world situation. . . . Whereas, the holistic person goes from the real world to the abstract and back, looking for analogies between the two tasks. At the end, both can achieve a more or less equal level of understanding. However, the steps that are taken to achieve the task are different" (Entwistle, 1981, 92; see also Tomlinson, 1984, 294ff).

On the other hand, although lacking conclusive evidence, the use of such expressions of different human qualities as impulsive-reflective cognitive styles, impressive, and independence-dependence, the result of works like that of Massari (1975) point to the existence of measurable individual differences. By this, we mean that there seem to clearly exist differences in the internal aspects of motivation that affect one's everyday conduct. There is no doubt that some individuals are field dependent and are more intense learners than are the field independent persons. They are more efficient learners under conditions of extrinsic motivation. The field independent learners, on the other hand, are more efficient learners under conditions of intrinsic motivation.

Further, the degree and quality of internal motivation depend on one's predisposition in reflectiveness or impulsiveness. One possible discriminating hypothesis for this lies in the differences in anxiety that has been detected as the steps are taken to solve a problem or complete a task. The anxiety generated in the reflective person may stem from the fact that mistakes can create feelings of incompetence. This person uses logic to minimize the possibility of making an error. In the case of the impulsive child, the anxiety is generated by both, the perception of incompetence and slowness, thereby tending to respond prematurely and thus increasing the possibility of making an error.

The fact remains that anxiety, even with different origins, shows up in both styles, causing some researchers to seek an answer as to why some individuals use strategies that are not too impulsive or too reflective (Kogan, 1981, p. 338). Perhaps, this is because reflectiveness and impulsiveness are no more than different ways to reason when confronted with a problem that elicits similar affective values. The pedagogical implication that can be derived from these deliberations is that instruction should be made more holistic so as to prevent the exaggeration of these differences in students. The different styles of mental processing are not to be taken lightly, but, as Carretero and Palacios (1982b, 102) say, they are more or less the forms used when confronted with tasks as well as forms of personality traits— considerations that can no longer be ignored.

Cognitive Styles and Hemisphericity. Different authors have been trying to establish a cognitive base. Sonnier and Goldsmith (in Sonnier, 1985a) have suggested that these forms of mental processes are related with cerebral hemispheric functions. True enough, the right hemisphere (in most people) is more related to the affective states as a preferred base for emotions; as well as the configuration of forms we see, movements in space, color which was probably the main way of thinking in early years of primitive man's individual development. It seems to have been the role of the right hemisphere during the evolutionary years of learning, prior to the creation of the symbolisms of language in man.

The existential, immediacy, subjectivity, mythical, simultaneous, and impulsiveness character of the primitive mind of the child may be good evidence for this. Today, this form of thinking keeps a close relationship with the learning style characteristic of the field dependent person: fast, impulsive, intuitive, global, and descriptive. It appears to have a relationship or resemblance with the perceptive visualizing method and the field dependent cognitive style. It is our opinion that the cognitive field independent person (whose characteristics are reflective, serious, cool, precise, and carefulness in mental operations) can be best associated with the analytical, realism, objectivity, deductive, rationality, and convergence of reality in abstraction that Sonnier and Goldsmith (Sonnier, 1985a) characterized as typical behavior of the left hemisphere; that of language, the dominant hemisphere of the species and its last conquest. This is the instrument that not only made it possible for man to translate past experiences to the present, but also to program and influence the future. Since language has its primary channel through audition, it stands to reason that it can also be called the auditive hemisphere.

When the child is four or five years old, he/she is an expert visualizer and begins to develop into and create his own image as a portion of the affective domain. This is the time in which the surrounding circumstances force him in an existential way from spontaneous words, the word-phrase, to the state of reflective reasoning, to coherent language, to more complex mental operations. It is the environment that awakens in him that potential for more powerful defensive strategies for coping with the constant threats against his individual differences. And, the child creates, lies, searches, tries things out, reflects, achieving in this manner the activation within himself/herself those potentials that are at the same time accumulating as personal rationality and mental habits. These mental habits develop in a determined number of children as they mature into their dominant learning processes. Some children maintain their primitive and spontaneous habits. These children perceive the environment visually and are yet to polarize the rational, analytical, linear-logical processes as a dominant characteristic. Actually, they have the freedom of more options in a time of confrontation. They process the external information, particularly in the scholastic environment, through the visual and/or the auditive channels.

Cognitive Style and Teaching Models. Conflicting arguments continue to emerge concerning a dichotomy in cognitive styles and the terminology and methodology of corresponding teaching styles. Which is best, to place students in the classroom of instructors with similar cognitive styles or to place them with instructors who have different styles? The truth is, we do not have sufficient empirical evidence with which to provide a conclusive answer. Stefano, in his doctoral dissertation, discussed the potential benefits that can come from instructor-student not necessarily having compatibility in cognitive styles. However, according to the better known works of Witkin (see Witkin, et al., 1977) field dependent students need to be more structured when being assisted through a lesson because of their own analytical shortcomings. Some of the student-teacher possibilities are:

1. Incompatibility in cognitive styles could bring about positive results.

2. The field dependent instructor tends to be a heavy user of the discussion method and may not be the best instructor to bring the structure needed by students, even those with the same cognitive style.

3.The heterogenity derived by teacher-student incompatibility in cognitive styles could introduce a dynamic interaction to the learning process (see also Packer and Bain, 1978).

We believe that there are two views concerning the fundamental characteristics of this dichotomy that should be considered. In education, one of the primary concerns should be the outstanding but ignored problem of scholastic failure. The cognitive style of the student and the selection of a teaching strategy should meet the needs of all students, each through his/her own dominant mode of perceiving, operating, and acting outside of the school. It is very important that at the initial contact between the student and the teacher, they should instantly tune in on the same wave length and use the same code of transmission and reception. Further, they should develop rapport so that the student can begin to develop his own potential in the subject matter at hand. The student's dominant cognitive style, along with subsequent scholastic aptitude differences, should be taxed and tested, but not beyond its limits.

As A. de la Garanderie (1983) suggested, the subject at hand should be treated as a second language and the child's language of speech be, in the learner's dominant cognitive style, "the pedagogic mother language," "visual" or "auditive," and it should be compatible with the learner's dominant style. Not to take this into account in teacher-student relationships can bring about "cognitive alienation" in some students. A teaching model that does not meet the needs of all students brings about atrophy of mental resources for some. They will resent and resist future scholastic activities before causing what Garanderie called "the feeling of being an outcast and becoming discouraged." In either case, directly or indirectly, the student is alienated, rejected, and becomes an academic outcast.

Less effective teaching methods do not take into consideration the mental development of all students. Some students are conditioned to diminish their potential as though they were handicapped from the onset. The damage produced is senseless when students are forced to function or cope in a different mode than their own native mode. They are placed at an unfair disadvantage. This produces not only a negative result, but anxiety as well.

Therefore, our conclusion is that holistic teaching strategies must be used so as to enrich a majority of students, each through his/her own thinking-learning mode. Interaction with the learning environment is facilitated so as to satisfy the curiosity and make achievement so easy as to proceed in a passive way rather than having to struggle for it.

There is yet another advantage to be gained by implementing holistic teaching strategies. Most important, it meets the needs of a heterogenous group of students with different cognitive styles. Holistic strategies, implemented as a teaching model, would all but eliminate the need for a massive testing program which prematurely separates students by their dominant mode of learning. Further, the implementation of holistic educational strategies provides the teacher with an excellent opportunity to more effectively exploit the potential talents of all students.

Without knowing or understanding these principles, some teachers achieve a high degree of success in their teaching styles and are like a May rain that benefits everyone. There are students that in rare cases seek to train themselves without much outside assistance and achieve a high degree of learning accomplishment for their own satisfaction. It is the knowledge of these facts that prompted the authors to investigate and attempt to understand these higher levels of achievement on the part of both teacher and learner.

In an attempt to study the relationship between *cognitive achievement* and pleasure in learning, *affective results*, the authors conducted an experiment with six teachers and 158 students of grades 6, 7, and 8. Six teachers were selected from among others whom had taken a test to determine their thinking/learning styles. Three of the selected teachers were self-declared as visually oriented persons (visualizers) and the other three were self-declared analytical persons (analyzers) (Sonnier, 1985b) (see Figure 18.1). Each had received training in the methods of holistic education at Santiago de Compostela (Galicia, Spain).

The investigation took place in 1985. For the experimental treatment, the students of these teachers were asked if they enjoyed a particular lesson, at its conclusion, and were asked to assess the amount that they had learned. These data were treated in four categories, 1 to 4 (from high to low) (see Sonnier and Santos Rego, 1984; Sonnier, 1985a; see Figure 18.2).

The three visual teachers and three analytically oriented teachers are listed, each with three class-groups that they taught in their normal ways of teaching (Group A, the control group) and to a second group they ad-

THINKING/LEARNING/SOCIAL STYLES

MOST PEOPLE USE ONE OF TWO BASIC WAYS OF THINKING, OR A
COMBINATION OF THE TWO. ON A SCALE OF 1 THROUGH 7,
SELECT THE EXPRESSION THAT BEST FITS YOUR OWN WAY OF THINKING

1 = VERY ANALYTICAL, LINEAR-LOGICAL, RATIONAL
(You line up your thoughts and reason them out)

7 = VERY VISUAL, HOLISTIC, INTUITIVE, CONFIGURATIONAL
(You can see the bits and pieces fall into the big picture)

4 = EQUAL USE OF BOTH WAYS

1. ANALYTICAL							VISUAL
(check	1	2	3	4	5	6	7
one)	( )	( )	( )	( )	( )	( )	( )

2. LOGICAL							HOLISTIC
(check	1	2	3	4	5	6	7
one)	( )	( )	( )	( )	( )	( )	( )

3. RATIONAL							INTUITIVE
(check	1	2	3	4	5	6	7
one)	( )	( )	( )	( )	( )	( )	( )

4. LINEAR-LOGICAL							CONFIGURATIVE
(check	1	2	3	4	5	6	7
one)	( )	( )	( )	( )	( )	( )	( )

5. CONSTRUCTIVE							CREATIVE
(check	1	2	3	4	5	6	7
one)	( )	( )	( )	( )	( )	( )	( )

6. RESERVE							ASSERTIVE
(check	1	2	3	4	5	6	7
one)	( )	( )	( )	( )	( )	( )	( )

7. UNSURE							CONFIDENT
(check	1	2	3	4	5	6	7
one)	( )	( )	( )	( )	( )	( )	( )

FIGURE 18.1

FOUR CATEGORIES OF COGNITIVE
ACHIEVEMENT/AFFECTIVE ATTAINMENT

(A) COGNITIVE ACHIEVEMENT	(B) AFFECTIVE ATTAINMENT
1. STUDENTS LEARNED A LOT	AND ENJOYED THE LESSON A LOT
2. STUDENTS LEARNED A LOT	BUT DID NOT ENJOY THE LESSON
3. STUDENTS DID NOT LEARN MUCH	BUT ENJOYED THE LESSON
4. STUDENTS DID NOT LEARN MUCH	AND DID NOT ENJOY THE LESSON

FIGURE 18.2

ministered holistic strategies (Group B, the experimental groups). In each case an objective grade was earned by each student, displayed in its sum or aggregate scores (Σ) for both treatment groups, as well as the mean for both of these scores ($\bar{X}$). These are the regular scores earned or achieved as a part of the subject matter learning process of the students and are the scores used for the purpose of reporting the academic progress of students.

The assessment made in this study was to determine the difference (B-A), between Treatment Group A and Treatment B, i.e., which treatment had advantage over the other. Because Category 1 of the four subjective categories is the one that indicates the highest level of achievement, comparisons are made in the differences between the first category for the two treatment groups. A positive result favors the holistic method. A negative value favors the traditional teaching method (see Table 18.1).

The teachers that participated in the investigation (first column) are listed (indicating their "Mode of Consciousness" as self-declared visualizer (5-7) or analyzer (1-3) (see Figure 18.1). *Group A* = a class taught by each teacher according to each's own teaching style (the mode of consciousness is an indication of preference of teaching style). *Group B* = the experimental group, each teacher administered holistic educational strategies to a second class. *Objective grades* = the grades earned by students in the normal testing and grading process, provided with Sum (Σ) and Group Average ($\bar{X}$). *Subjec-*

TABLE 18.1
OBJECTIVE AND SUBJECTIVE RESULTS
OF HOLISTIC EDUCATIONAL STRATEGIES

TEACHERS   STUDENTS

VISUALIZERS		NUMBER OF STUDENTS PER TEACHER	GROUP "A"						GROUP "B"						DIFFERENCES B-A		
			COGNITIVE ACHIEVEMENT		AFFECTIVE CATEGORY				COGNITIVE ACHIEVEMENT		AFFECTIVE CATEGORY				COGNITIVE ACHIEVEMENT		AFFECTIVE ACHIEVEMENT IN THE FIRST CATEGORY
			Σ	X̄	1	2	3	4	Σ	X̄	1	2	3	4	Σ	X̄	
	$1^{(7)}$	27	81	3.00	24	0	3	0	95	3.52	25	0	2	0	14	0.52	1
	$2^{(6)}$	18	31	1.72	3	3	11	1	35	1.94	7	3	7	1	4	0.22	4
	$3^{(6)}$	27	55	2.04	7	2	8	10	57	2.11	10	8	6	3	2	0.07	3
Σ	3	72	167	2.31	34	5	22	11	187	2.60	42	11	15	4	20	0.28	8
ANALYZERS																	
	$1^{(3)}$	23	50	2.17	1	8	11	3	50	2.17	7	5	11	0	0	0.00	8
	$2^{(2)}$	26	55	2.21	1	21	2	2	53	2.04	19	2	5	0	-2	-0.08	18
	$3^{(2)}$	37	78	2.11	1	6	26	4	89	2.40	24	2	9	2	11	0.29	23
Σ	3	86	183	2.13	3	35	39	9	192	2.23	50	9	25	3	9	0.10	47
Σ	6	158	350	2.21	37	40	61	20	379	2.40	92	20	40	7	29	0.18	55

tive estimate = criterion provided by students on a scale of 1 to 4 (from high to low, see Figure 17.3, p. 129). The subjective estimates are criteria assignments by students about the class taught. *Subjective Estimate in the First Criterion* = the highest criterion, the students learned a lot and enjoyed the lesson a lot.

The difference between the group mean scores made on the test at the end of the subject matter lesson was 0.28 in favor of the visually oriented teachers and a less impressive 0.10 for the anlytically oriented teachers. However, the report of affective involvement by the students is significant. For the visual teachers the aggregate score for category 1 was 8 points of difference between treatment groups, in favor of holistic teaching. And, for the analytical teacher the score was an impressive 47 points of difference in category 1.

There were 72 students in the three visual teachers' classes and 86 in the analytical teachers' classes, for a total of 158 students. The gain for the entire sample in subject matter achievement scores was 0.18 in favor of the holistic educational treatment of the experimental groups. And, there was reported a high degree of enjoyment (at the rate of 55 points in favor of the same treatment group).

Therefore, in the academic achievement grades as well as the subjective estimation, or affective involvement, it is evident that the holistic oriented mode of classroom management was of benefit not just to most students but very likely to all of them. Its implementation would appear to be an invaluable tool for academic as well as for social progress in the total welfare of students. The real contribution of holistic strategies as a model for wide-spread implementation is that it does not favor one or the other of the cognitive styles of individual differences among learners. It is therefore imperative that it be implemented for the purpose of providing good instruction at all levels and disciplines because of the benefits that can be reaped by all students.

PART VI

INSTRUCTIONAL STRATEGIES
THAT PROMOTE AFFECTIVE RESULTS

Craig A. Buschner, Editor

There are many ways to vary a lesson plan so as to provide the added spices of affective learning. Among others, a few strategies are given as examples of ways to elicit affective results (quality learning). These are: the use of simulators (CHAPTER 19), values clarification and moral development (CHAPTER 20), role playing (CHAPTER 21), the sharing of visual expressions to reinforce the highlights of a unit or lesson (CHAPTER 22), and writing across the curriculum, which means some writing in all subjects (CHAPTER 23).

C.A.B.

THE USE OF CULTURE SIMULATOR VIGNETTES AS A TEACHING DEVICE

Frank F. Montalvo

Twenty-six vignettes were so constructed as to depict incidents of inter-cultural misunderstandings often encountered by Hispanics (see Chapter 10 for more details on the construction and application of the cultural simula-tor). They get at the heart of differences that often surface between a non-Hispanic counselor and Hispanic clients. The vignettes differ in their struc-ture from case studies commonly used in parallel teaching objectives. A major difference is that in constructing the vignettes, essential information required to arrive at an accurate assessment is omitted in order to reveal the reader's implicit framework for interpreting a variety of intercultural experiences.

Intercultural encounters that have the potential for misunderstandings be-come problematic when the reader is asked to identify the source of a problem from among three or four reasonable explanations. The vignettes were pre-pared to motivate Social Work trainees to discuss the probable cause of a particular behavior in question, and to identify the probable sources and to provide alternate explanations.

For each vignette, one explanation attributes the source of the problem to a culturally-specific set of values, attitudes, or beliefs underlying the be-havior. Too, the vignette may elicit a mind-set, based on on the trainee's experience with ethnic, minority groups. For most of the explanations that are elicited, an intercultural attribution is the inferred cause of culturally influenced behavior (Brislin, 1981). The remaining explanations are misattributions based on commonly held tenets of what constitutes *appropriate human behavior, accepted principles of therapeutic intervention*, or *stereotypic perceptions of hispanic people*. None of the latter attributions provide an accurate assessment of the problem depicted in any of the vignettes.

Role play of the incidents by the students is preferred when the vignette provides sufficient descriptive details. Any of the vignettes may be read to the class with the entire group entering into a discussion of the explanations. A more fruitful, but time consuming approach, is to divide the class into small groups and provide each group with one of several vignettes covering the same subject. This is the recommended approach. The group process used by the students in attacking the problem is similar to the one they would experience at an initial case conference in an agency or clinic.

Three to six vignettes are included under each of the six subject modules presented in the present set of experiences in order to enrich the class discussion with the multiple dimensions of the subject. Following a suitable period of discussion in order to determine the relative accuracy of the explanations, the students rate their answers by priority: from the most likely to the least likely attribution for the behavior. At this point, the instructor provides the student groups with a copy of the rationales for the extent to which the answers were accurate or inaccurate. They should be read in the order that the students selected their answers. Not all correct answers are those that appear to address the cultural value, since the students can also err in attributing behavior to "the culture" when it is due to other factors.

Accordingly, much of the teaching value of the vignettes rests in the thorough discussion of all of the alternative explanations and in the students' comparing the reasons for their selections with those provided in the rationales.

Also, the case synopses were not designed to provide complete information for the students to arrive at a satisfactory solution in each vignette. Rather, the purpose was to introduce the sociocultural variable as the best choice among the selections provided and the information concerning the incident. Other explanations are possible, depending on the relative weight that is given to additional information that is obtained about the actors in the vignette. In order for the students to improve their ability to analyze the relative impact of psychological, social, and cultural factors on individuals, they should consider the additional information that they would need to confirm either the "correct" answer or any alternate explanations. The misunderstanding that took place in some of the vignettes is due precisely to one counselor's failure to obtain additional information from the client.

The text that precedes and follows each vignette, or set of vignettes, provides a guide for the instructor to lead an open class discussion as the theoretical and practical implications of the conclusions the student groups reached in their deliberations. Discussion of current research findings bearing on the topic and suggestions for additional learning activities are provided. The references are a source of supplementary reading. The text also suggests the appropriate arrangement of vignettes into pairs or subsets within each subject module for optimum class and group discussion.

Every vignette focuses on one central theme or value, although other values are sub-themes in the vignette and may constitute teaching points of special interest to the instructor. For example, the role of grandparents in extended families may be taught by combining the vignette concerned with the Spanish language with those aimed at presenting the continued authority of the grandfather in the family. The 26 vignettes and the accompanying narrative, however, were arranged for cumulative learning and for increased understanding and ability to solve cross-cultural problems. Each subset was anticipated to take at least one hour of thorough teaching and learning. Such factors as size and composition of the class, student's prior experience and training, and the instructor's teaching objectives also influence the time allotted for this activity.

The original vignettes were constructed to be arranged in a self-teaching series for implementation without the benefit of additional instruction or discussion. A similar plan may be used by the instructor if the objective is to provide an economical method of orienting large numbers of trainees to Hispanic values, life-styles, and problems. The vignette becomes an instrument that is easily administered and scored. However, this application mode is discouraged. The author's experience, confirmed by a survey of users of the original "culture simulator," indicates that this approach may serve to confound and confuse, rather than to be helpful. By its very nature, the use of vignettes as a testing instrument raises many unanswerable questions for the trainees, does not provide them with the opportunity to integrate this approach, nor does it allow for them to work through the feelings that are provoked by the vignettes. Consideration of alternate interventions and consolidation of theoretical implications are also curtailed by this application mode.

Along this line, transferring the culture simulator's self-teaching format into a computer program suffers from similar limitations and may render the materials too expensive for general public access. Such a development awaits the construction of an interactive program where the students' individual learning styles are incorporated as each of the issues raised above are addressed.

In any case, whether in writing or on a computer terminal, a programmed approach severely limits the flexibile use of the materials by the instructor and the elaboration of the text with personal experiences, anecdotal references, and special instructional objectives. It also limits the instructor's ability to deal with the students' academic preparation to accept and assimilate the new information, which may often appear inconsistent with their own cherished values, norms, and beliefs.

There is a postscript to the use of the culture simulator as a teacher-training device. The author conducted a survey about a year after being used as an instrument of self-instruction. It was found that among the 50 trainers sampled, only 3/50 (6%) were still using the vignettes in that manner and technique. It was found that the rest of the trainers and teachers were using vignettes as case studies to motivate discussion. This was one of the factors that prompted the writing of these comments about the use of simulator vignettes as a teaching device. As with the original intent and purpose, the extended strategies and techniques herein described could just as well be applicable to teacher education of other areas and disciplines.

CHAPTER 20

VALUES CLARIFICATION AND MORAL DEVELOPMENT IN FAMILY LIFE EDUCATION

David R. Stronck

American teachers overwhelmingly support sex education in both secondary and elementary schools. Most teachers approve the discussion of such topics as the biology of reproduction, venereal disease, and birth control in high school. And, where sex education is taught, they approve topics that involve more value judgments: e.g., premarital sex, abortion, and homosexuality. For elementary schools, the only topic to receive majority approval was the biology of reproduction, the topic most remote from values involvement (Gallup, 1985). A broader curriculum, beyond reproduction education, termed "Family Life Education," is in the process of being used either with or as replacement for "Sex Education." New Jersey, among the first states to require family life education, defined its comprehensive program (1981), in this way:

> Instruction to develop an understanding of the physical, mental, emotional, social, economic, and psychological aspects of interpersonal relationships; the physiological, psychological, and cultural foundations of human development, sexuality, and reproduction at various stages of growth; the opportunity for pupils to acquire knowledge which will support the development of responsible personal behavior, strengthen their own family life now, and aid in establishing strong family life for themselves in the future, thereby contributing to the enrichment of the community (Hendrixson, 1981).

Progress has been slow and difficult. Kirby, Alter, and Scales (1979) have estimated that a mere 10% of the nation's teenagers are ever exposed to such a comprehensive course. The problem seems to stem from the opposition of parents who fear that educational programs in schools will attack their values. Teachers have supported sex education programs in schools because they believe that such programs are designed only to *clarify* values, not to change them. Further, Gordon, Scales, and Everly (1979) have offered evidence that sexuality education courses do not lead youngsters away from their parents' values.

At the heart of this matter, Amonker (1980) observed that peers are the major source of sex information for adolescents, while teachers and school counselors are rarely regarded as a major source. In general, communication about human sexuality has unfortunately been left to chance, myths, superstitions, and the media. The only conclusion that can be drawn is that many parents have incorrectly assumed that their children will acquire the parents' values about sex, despite an almost total silence on the topic. Yet, one of the greatest advantages of sexuality education in the schools has been the encouragement of greater communication between children and their parents.

Some of the credit for this impact may be due to teaching strategies that have been used. Two among the various techniques, *values clarification* and *moral development*, should be mentioned in that they obtain high levels of cognitive achievement while at the same time promote affective results. In that the *values clarification* technique has been met with some resistance, a second technique has been offered. Both are worthy of a closer look.

Values Clarification. One strategy to open the discussion in the values clarification technique is to have each person identify something said or done in the last 24 hours, "that you are proud of." Another strategy for opening discussion is to "name favorite things, or to list gifts that you most want." The rest depends on the instructor's skills in converting from a discussion leader to a facilitator in promoting the flow of ideas from the entire group. Because values clarification is a system of strategies, it is intended to be neutral toward promoting any one value. Some of the organized opponents of sex education programs complain against values clarification because it seems to allow students excessive freedom to choose among various alternatives.

In cases where the technique has been questioned, there was in all probility a violation of the original intent. Simon and Olds (1977), explain that moralizing, manipulating, and modeling do not help children in learning to analyze confusing ideas and situations and to decide on what to do. Moralizing tends to block genuine communication. And, manipulation by reward and punishment does not help youngsters to weigh the pros and cons, nor to decide issues on their merits. Also, in determining sources of values for youth, modeling has become increasingly difficult in our society. Each child usually has many models: father, mother, older brothers and sisters, clergymen, teacher, scout leader, friend, television star, and sports hero. The intent of values clarification is to provide strategies for dealing democratically with values in our multicultural, and multi-religious public schools, thus meeting the needs of different students in our complex society.

Moral Development. Kohlberg (1973) offered the Cognitive Moral Development approach to values and moral education. This approach includes strategies that stimulate students to move toward higher stages of moral reasoning. He has identified *six stages of moral reasoning*, the highest (and sixth stage) being ethical decisions that are derived from logical, universal, and consistent principles, e.g., as the Golden Rule. Moral dilemma discussion has been effective in leading to these stages of growth. Certainly sexuality education, as one of the topics of family life education, may include many topics for dilemma discussions. For example, when is it permissible for a pregnant woman to elect an abortion? These discussions are fertile in providing informed reasoning for either side of the issue, as well as an understanding of why another individual should want to have an opposing view. Kohlbergians believe that values clarification stops short with self-awareness. They advocate direct discussion by the teacher toward arriving at behaviors that are part of our American tradition and heritage, e.g., respect and love for individuals. Without violating the religious beliefs or cultural attitudes within our democracy, the public schools can present the common moral values expressed and implied in the Declaration of Independence and in the U.S. Constitution.

The values involved in sex education programs tend to be very conservative, traditional, and universally acceptable. Some examples demonstrating such values are the following:

The Illinois Sex Education Act (McNab, 1981) includes the following objectives:

> To realize that the Golden Rule also applies in sexual matters, based upon the ethical principle that no one has the right to harm another by using him or her exploitatively as a sex object.

> To learn about the dangers of illicit sexual behavior, and that boys and girls do not have to engage in heavy petting or premarital sexual intercourse to make friends, be popular, get dates, or to prove their love and affection to each other.

> To emphasize the case for premarital chastity as the sexual standard approved by our society because chastity provides a positive goal for teenagers, linking human sexual behavior with love, marriage, parenthood, and family life and because of the individual, family and community problems associated with premarital or extramarital sexual relations.

Among the basic principles of moral education recognized by the Salt Lake City Schools are these (Gordon, 1981):

> Each individual has dignity and worth.

> A free society requires respect for persons, property and principles.

> Each individual is responsible for his or her own actions.

The National Education Department of Planned Parenthood Federation of America has adopted the following as some of the values that underlie contemporary sexuality education (Scales, 1982):

> Sexual decisions should support the dignity, equality, and worth of each individual.

> It is wrong to force or exploit someone into an unwanted sexual experience, to knowingly spread disease, or to bring an unwanted child into the world.

> Parenthood requires many responsibilities that adolescents are usually unable to assume and capabilities they usually do not have.

Leading Discussions. Advocates of either Values Clarifications or Cognitive Moral Development recommend creating a classroom atmosphere of open and active discussion. Young people discuss sexual information especially with their peers. They should be able to conduct these discussions in a classroom with responsible adults. The teacher then can correct misinformation and encourage the clear recognition of the consequences of some actions. Alternative behaviors can be analyzed especially to eliminate any that violate the moral values expressed or implied in the Declaration of Independence and the U.S. Constitution.

Bignell (1982) explained how the discussion technique allows students to share facts and ideas, while at the same time clarifying their own feelings and values. Informed students, perhaps following a lecture, film, reading assigment, or guest speaker, are more apt to evoke input and get more out of student discussions. Thus, the activity requires adequate planning with good questions to stimulate participation. Further, he suggested questions that involve values and moral dilemmas, including:

How important is virginity in this day and age?

What should be the purpose of sex?

What is the double standard? Does it still exist?

What are the pros and cons of premarital sex?

What does it mean to "use" someone sexually?

How important are love, affection, caring, honesty, and respect to a sexual relationship?

Sometimes students are not ready to speak openly in the classroom about such topics. Another strategy is to invite students to write questions anonymously on cards. Teachers can then answer the questions and encourage discussion after giving basic responses. If a class is large, teachers can divide the students into smaller groups for discussion. Each "buzz group" should have four or five students who work for a limited time with specific instructions.

Conclusion. Most states require written permission from the parents before teachers can begin dealing with topics of sexuality education. When communicating with parents, teachers should explain that a major goal of the school program is to encourage discussion and a sharing of values between parents and their children. Discussion in the classroom that involves values can be directed toward eliminating behavior that contradict the common moral values expressed by the Declaration of Independence and the U.S. Constitution. Teachers can be most active by allowing an atmosphere for open and active discussion.

CHAPTER 21

PAINTING THE CLASSROOM
WITH THE REALITY OF ROLE PLAYING

Linda Kay

As Joan Miro, with just a few lines, could make a statement in a painting, so can a teacher, with just a few strokes, transform a classroom into another place. By rearranging the chairs, the classroom becomes a court room, a Senate chamber, or a subcommittee hearing room. With a black robe and a gavel, a student is transformed into a Supreme court judge.

The following scenarios took place in a high school, but could just as well apply for other levels of education. One rule to remember in beginning role play is that no student is to play a role or do anything that he/she does not want to do. This way, the teacher remains free to make suggestions. If the student chooses to do something different, the teacher should not force the issue. Indeed, the students are told to follow their own instincts of right or wrong because they have to take the responsibility for their decisions, by statements such as: "Do only what is comfortable for you and what you feel like doing. If I ask you to do something and you don't want to, trust your own feelings and tell me. It will probably turn out just as well—maybe even better."

Simulating Events and Role Playing. Following a study on how bills become a law, my class enacted a Senate subcommittee hearing. This simulation was of the hearing before the U.S. Senate Subcommittee on Public

Works which resulted in the enactment of the 55 Miles Per Hour speed limit law. The game taught the students many things. Among them was the amount of information that is needed to enact a proposal into law and how emotionally involved individuals (independent truckers, for instance) can get during debate over a bill.

Getting the Students Involved. The roles were typed out for each witness and the facts pertinent to the bill were listed on individual role sheets. The students were encouraged to choose their role from the following: one of the senators on the subcommittee, a witness, or one of the members of the press or senate staff. Each student usually had a role to play, but in the very large classes, there would not be enough to go around. In that case, everyone had an opportunity to ask questions of the witnesses or senators during the discussion following each witness' testimony. Witnesses included a Teamsters Union representative, an American Automobile Association executive, the Secretary of Transportation, a trucking executive, a State Highway Department executive, a public interest group representative, and others.

The Nature of the Involement. The four "Senators" represented a New England state, a Western state, a Southern state, and a Great Plains state. They asked questions determined by their constituents' situations. Very quickly, the students got into actual debate on the subject. The roles were simply a starting point at which the students can become involved in the issues. They gave them some of the basic facts to argue for or against. Most of my classes were able to digest the facts and carry on the debate from their own realms of experience and knowledge, once the process was underway.

The materials for this particular simulation game were developed when the 55 Mile Per Hour speed limit was first enacted into law in 1976 and it continues to be a useful model. Over the years, the discussions resulted in varying degrees of sympathy with the law, depending upon the availability of gasoline at the time the game was played.

Getting Students Personally Involved. I found that once a debate got going, the students tended to forget their roles and began to debate from their own perspectives, which I did not think was bad. The students felt free to tell me if there was a problem of getting into and out of their roles. We discussed this and after each day's games, we spent time discussing the feelings each person had while in the role and how their feelings affected his/her reaction to the debates.

Other Ways of Simulation and Role Playing. Supreme Court cases were reinacted to achieve lessons learned on the here-and-now level. One short drama was read aloud by students who played roles of the justices at the hearing which studied Richard Nixon and the supression of the Watergate tapes. Each student, whether reading a role or not, was asked to pretend that he/she was a Supreme Court judge. They listened to Leon Jawarski's and James D. St. Clair's arguments and then sat as one of the eight justices who heard the U.S. vs Nixon case. We reviewed Article Two, Section 2 of the Constitution, dealing with powers of the President.

Working in groups of four or five, the students reviewed both sides of the arguments presented and then considered their own ideas and beliefs regarding law and justice. Finally, they reached a decision and discussed their reasoning. We compared each group's decisions, discussed them, and then compared our decisions with what the "real court" had decided.

In another kind of simulation game, I had the students play roles related to a New City Telephone Company in which each group had five members—four vice presidents and a president. Goals for each company were set at the beginning of the game. During the game, students made decisions concerning various policies, such as whether to install electronic switching in certain areas, salary and vacation decisions, productivity decisions and what to do about profit and loss or inflation. The team that made the most points was the team which had stuck most closely to their pre-set goals in the beginning of the game.

The competition to get the most points was strong, as points were tallied at the end of several rounds. "Company members" had to rely on each other to help the company make good decisions, keeping in mind the goals they originally set for themselves. After the game, we talked about the feelings the students had as team members, and whether or not it made any difference in their decisions, or whether they made their decisions on their own.

Dealing With Sensitivity and Hurt—Building Trust. While discussing the problem of cheating in school one day, I let the students role play scenarios of different alternatives. We discussed how hostility of a friend who was cheating came out when the friend was "ratted on", and how to deal with this. After the roles had been played, breaking class rules or keeping friendships intact were also discussed. Every person made their own decisions based on how they really felt.

At the school we had a number of foreign students, mainly from Central America, who lived in on-campus dormitories. One day we were role playing a civil suit in which a foreign student had been "accused" of making "untoward advances" on an American girl, resulting in her "getting mononucleosis." She was "suing for payment of her doctor bills."

When students really got personally involved in a role, it was sometimes difficult to know what would result. The "attorneys" for the "plaintiff" were unprepared for the "defendant's" argument that there was a cultural difference between the two parties. In Honduras, he pointed out, people are much more publicly affectionate: touching other people is not such a big deal that it is in Mississippi. This point brought out some very strong feelings. The turn of events in this case, based on this cultural difference, decided the jurors in favor of the defendant, but not before the opposing "attorneys" had voiced strong feelings toward each other.

The feelings were so strong, in fact, that I "froze" the actions, de-roled everyone, and had them reassign the roles and started the trial all over again. After the second trial, the two girls who had both played the role of the first opposing attorneys, were still highly emotional. They had difficulty getting out of their roles. To my relief, before class the next morning, the two girls came to me, arms around each other, to tell me that they had talked about their feelings and decided that they wanted to be on the same side the next time they argued a case!

I asked the foreign student who had been the defendant in this firey case how he had felt during the trial. He said, "I felt afraid at first because they did not understand me, but I was able to explain how it was in my country and I know that I was right. I felt good that I was able to make them see how it is there. Then, I wasn't afraid anymore."

Conclusion. The obvious result and impact of role playing are high degrees of both cognitive achievement and affective attainment. However, in my estimation, there are other qualities in the area of affective education to impact from this strategy. Very important skills can be taught to improve trust between people. Trust is a basic dimension of human life and has many aspects: openness, honesty, dependability, predictability, love, protection, and acknowledgement. It is a dimension fundamental to all social interactions, even to role-defined behavior. But within formal roles, trust has an institutional component which is usually lacking in informal behavior (i.e., one gains trust by effectively carrying out a role).

The best technique for creating trust in a class is to build a link between people. This can take many forms: establishing a talking relationship, creating a work-role relationship, creating an experiential relationship (i.e., different people experiencing something at the same time and place). The relationship thus established must be a predictable one and individuals must then act according to expectation.

CHAPTER 22

SHARING VISUAL EXPERIENCES

Isadore L. Sonnier

Sharing visual experiences offers a change of pace opportunity and is an excellent enrichment activity. It incorporates holistic strategies in that it employs a multimedia approach and has multisensural applicability. As one of the culminating activities of a lesson or unit, the students are asked to relive the experiences of that lesson, and to list the major ideas that were presented. They are to abstract these major ideas through a picture, a poster, or a visual expression *that says it all*. For example, they will extract the highlights and major ideas and determine a theme for these ideas. This theme will then be made into a graphic display that is to be shared with the rest of the class.

Initiating the Activity. Arrange for the students to meet in groups of three- or four-member discussion teams. THE ASSIGNMENT: 1) Discuss what we have learned; 2) Make a list of the major ideas; 3) Determine a theme that conveys all, or at least a broad segment of the lesson; and, 4) Draw a visual expression *that says it all* about the theme. This visual expression is to be shared with the class. Allow a few minutes for the discussion to evolve into the internal organization and structure that normally follows in group interactions. Then, just in case the process needs prodding, announce the second task: "Appoint someone in your group to make a list of the major ideas that you have learned." As each group gets underway with this task and several ideas are listed, announce the third task by either pointing out the location of the materials, or distribute the materials yourself, taking the opportunity to personally observe these processes in each group.

Materials Needed:

1) Colored crayons and/or felt pens.

2) Poster paper or sheets of newsprint paper.

(NOTE: Your local newspaper will let you have for the asking the unused ends of newsprint paper rolls.)

Depending on the teacher's strategy, a spokesperson for each group is either appointed by the teacher or selected by the team. Each group is asked to share their theme or the essence of their discussions with the rest of the class. In the course of these small group proceedings, the students' feelings and sensitivities are often deeply exposed. Therefore, in these proceedings, as well as in the class activities to follow, it may be necessary to remind them to respect each other's ideas. Each person's ideas are to be valued. "Try to make only positive and contributing comments and keep other remarks to yourselves." Understandably, senseless and careless remarks could destroy these activities.

When the students have exhausted their list of important ideas learned, and are well into the selection and execution of their composite visual expression, select or allow the first group to volunteer. Generally, these presentations are made by one person, voicing the group's recapulative expression and another person holds up their graphic impression or visual expression in display.

It may be notably difficult to do this activity for the first few times. Students usually do not have the social and artistic skills readily available to flow into this activity smoothly. However, repeated opportunities provide students with the obvious need and incentive to sharpen these skills. Indeed, social and artistic skills flow as natural by-products of this activity. Also, this is an excellent way to reinforce the content taught.

While *sharing visual experiences* cannot be done at the conclusion of all learning experiences, it certainly makes a nice change-of-pace activity. More important, these are holistic strategies in that both of the cerebral hemispheres are simultaneously and concurrently stimulated. And, few can doubt the potential and fertility of this activity for student growth and development in both visual and analytical skills. Maybe not at first, however, in time this activity also yields a heavy potential for attaining positive affective results. It is important to note that some classes resist doing this activity at first and it may take as many as five to ten experiences before the necessary leadership qualities emerge and the graphics arts skills are sufficiently developed to have smooth and meaningful sessions of *sharing visual experiences.*

A latent objective for doing this activity on a regular basis is the fact that leadership skills are developed. The domineering and submissive tendencies of individuals become secondary and subordinate to individuals' thoughts and talents, as each individual becomes one of the team members. These personal and social skills begin to emerge in the process. And, the affective results soar.

CHAPTER 23

WRITING ACROSS THE CURRICULUM INCREASES THE OPPORTUNITY FOR ACADEMIC EXCELLENCE

Claudine B. Sonnier

As a classroom teacher, I am constantly looking for methods of teaching that will get the maximum performance from each student and will require the minimal amount of grading time. The most challenging and innovative method in my classroom has been a program commonly called Writing Across the Curriculum (WAC). This simply means writing in all subjects and at all levels of learning. In proper perspective, writing is a lifelong developmental process, and along with reading, it is fundamental to one's level of literacy. When managed correctly, writing is not only a means towards affective education, but also develops many talents. Among these are *academic competence, creativity, planning and organizing skills,* and the most obvious which is the development of *communications skills.*

This list makes one aware that academic competence is but one of the talents which should be developed and not necessarily the most important one. I am of the opinion that WAC fosters the development of all of these vital skills simultaneously and concurrently. For example, when writing, a person must plan, create, and communicate. If given more frequent exposure to writing opportunities, the student develops the ability to go beyond linear-logical reasoning and put together seemingly unrelated information in coming up with new solutions and new sensitivity to problems.In addition to and concurrent with this broad spectrum of talent development, writing also allows for affective attainment to soar. Allowing time for writing helps learning to become pleasurable, especially for those students who do not usually have a high success record. Writing during class is not to be interpreted as copying of facts. In writing about any subject, the student should be allowed to evaluate, criticize, and summarize the subject. When allowed to criticize, the subject is learned with little effort and the student often finds, as nowhere else in the curriculum, a great outlet for pent up emotions.

It is my belief that WAC, or writing in every classroom, has untold advantages to both student and teacher. Isn't every teacher happy and of high self-esteem when students are working happily and making progress toward the established goals and expectations? I would like to share the seven reasons why I have students write in Home Economics classes.

1. *Writing keeps everyone on task.* When writing is presented as a happy experience, students enjoy being busy. If writing is praised and shared with others, working and learning becomes joyful and full of excitement. The age old problem of "keeping everyone on task" is all but eliminated because intensive writing demands holistic concentration.

2. *Writing reinforces learning.* Of all the ways to reinforce learning, writing is one of the best. The students who write an explanation of how something is done, writes to explain reasons for, or beliefs about an incident or established fact, and are allowed to share this with fellow students understand the subject better than those students who are only required to list answers or identify the correct answer from multiple choice groupings. As a student places on paper these marks and symbols, which we call writing, in order to tell others what he/she knows, he/she must relate with, and thus develop a unique understanding of the subject. In planning, creating and communicating through the writing process, he/she gets new and personally involved insights. While using written words as tools to explore, analyze and explain a subject, the writer develops insight into the subject matter that is unequal or unmatched elsewhere.

3. *Writing promotes group understanding.* Every student is from a different background because of cultural, economic, educational, and attitudinal differences in past experiences. Therefore no two students are exactly alike

in the way they view a problem, situation or experience. Sometimes these differences are outstanding and the so-called weak or timid student may show depth and wisdom which comes as a surprise to both teacher and classmates. My experience is that when students are allowed time-in-class not only to write, but to also share with each other what they have written, an understanding bond is developed between fellow classmates. Thus, while writing to learn the subject, the student is also becoming wiser about the differences among peers that exist in our melting-pot culture. This wisdom, seldom an objective in the traditional curriculum, should help prepare students for happier and more fulfilling roles in our society.

4. *Writing helps students learn about themselves.* In writing, students discover themselves. Experiences are combined with thoughts, feelings, and knowledge that are interwoven into new meaning. Since language is a tool of one's analytical and visual processes, a writer becomes a part of what is written as he/she analyzes and personalizes these new meanings into a language which is to be read by someone else. The students have often reported that when writing without fear of being graded, ideas flow and become written which were not previously known about oneself. This appears to be a common experience when, as a part of a classroom experience, students are allowed to write freely. Ungraded journal writing is great for this type of writing. Students are also encouraged to write about favorite or unfavorite family members, or pleasant or unpleasant life experiences. Interviewing family members—especially older people, and writing about the interview is another way of gaining self-knowledge. It is important that students know more, not only about the subject, but about themselves, as well.

5. *Writing makes learning fun.* Learning does not have to be a chore. Neither does writing. Students should look forward to coming to class knowing that the time spent there will not be the memorizing of uninteresting facts. Writing should never be used as punishment. Why destroy the natural inclination to put things on paper by making writing something done for punishment? Instead, writing can make learning a much more exciting experience.

6. *Writing raises self-esteem.* When students are allowed to write and share, they begin to feel better about themselves. This is shown in several ways which I have noticed in my classes. As self-esteem goes up, so does academ-

ic performance—thus, grades. Students become more open and begin to overcome shyness, school is an exciting place to be, learning is pleasurable, and class attendance is improved. The greatest reward for teacher and students is that students who feel good about themselves spend their time learning and present fewer discipline problems.

7. *Keeping a Journal Makes Writing Fun.* Students at any level in any class are usually delighted to keep a journal. The materials are simple: a spiral notebook, pen or pencil, and six minutes at the beginning or end of class. Students do best when the teacher promises not to read the secrets. This might sound without purpose, but it is one more opportunity to practice making marks and symbols which are writing, to organize thoughts and ideas, and to record them.

Implementing the Program. Several questions emerge as to how the teacher can have students to write more, write with meaning and depth, and to present writing as a pleasurable activity. Basic to all of these questions and in terms of affective education, it is important that writing in all subjects be a happy experience, not just "added on busy work." Through trial and error and repeated experiences, just like learning to talk, students learn to write a story as they explain how to work a math problem, explain a chemistry or biology laboratory experiment, or write to explain the current use and purpose of a typewriter or computer, sewing machine, or kitchen equipment. These are all everyday learning experiences that could include writing as an integral part of the total learning experience. The teachers, of course, must believe in what they are doing. And, they must be willing to either read some of the work, or to allow time for peer interaction. There must be a sounding board for exciting stories to be shared and even be warmly received.

In conclusion, it is well established that writing prepares students to communicate fluently on various personal, social, and occupational levels. Clearly, WAC helps schools to reach the ultimate goal of education: to develop literate, productive, and insightful citizens. The most remarkable thing about WAC is that these ends are met along with positive affective results. Both, quantity and quality educational objectives are met.

PART VII

AFFECTIVE RESULTS
IN DIFFERENT MODES OF TEACHING

Linda Kay, Editor

Obtaining affective results is not only possible, but flows quite naturally for teachers who practice in all three modes of teaching preferences: authoritarian (CHAPTER 24), eclectic (CHAPTER 25), and self-directed (CHAPTER 26). The contributions in these three chapters are from different teachers who have different motives and strategies. To put into practice a well known aphorism in a little known application, the authoritarian reaches the heart through the students' heads and the self-directed reaches the heads through the students' hearts. The eclectic teacher reaches for the best of both worlds.

L. K.

CHAPTER 24

EFFECTIVE AND AFFECTIVE ALGEBRA: AN AUTHORITARIAN VIEW

Tressie S. Harper

Algebra. *"I love algebra. It's my favorite subject."–"I hate algebra. It's a pain."* These are statements made by many students everywhere. Yes, there does seem to be a dichotomy of students' attitudes about algebra. More often than not, this attitude has its roots in the students' feelings about arithmetic in general. Mathematics is easy for some and difficult for others. Granted, hard work is a major factor to success in math, but some students do have an easier time of it. This may be attributed to brain hemisphere dominance for which holistic strategies may present far reaching solutions toward teaching/learning effectiveness. I share some of my concerns to insure this effectiveness when I teach algebra. The basic or primary concern I have is to maintain a proper balance between the students' cognitive development and affective attainment. The first, cognitive development comes as the student experiences success in mastering the skills. Hopefully, after I teach algebraic concepts, there will have been some advancement in both, cognitive achievement and the attainment of positive affective results. One affects the other. The skillful teacher must try to recognize the needs of the students in both aspects of growth. Needless to say, the psychomotor domain, my third area of primary concern, is necessary for the student to actually demonstrate the mastered skills for evaluation.

Some educators propose that the teacher must build the student's self-esteem first and then teach skills. My experience is that by learning algebraic skills thoroughly, the student will experience success. Nothing can build self-esteem as much as experiencing success in tasks. It could be compared to the chicken-or-egg-first debate. Which comes first, self-esteem or success? I say success.

When entering an algebra class, students bring pre-existing schemata about math. I try to lead the students to the fact that they should not close doors in their minds. I discourage "can't-itis" from the start. After having been given a thorough explanation, hard work on the part of the student is the only way to experience success. This means hard work in class as well as homework on a regular basis. Checking this homework in class and explaining missed problems is integral to the desired successful outcome.

Some students experience difficulty adapting to algebra because it differs from the arithmetic experiences of previous years. In arithmetic, the students are taught units of skills. If a student does poorly in the unit on subtraction, there is the chance of doing better when a new unit on multiplication is introduced. One experience does not necessarily relate to the next. However, in the first course of algebra, the skills are learned in a sequence. There are prerequisite skills which lead on to more complex skills. If the students do not master early skills, trouble is ahead. Each skill is used repeatedly throughout the course. The course is by nature linear-logically structured and must be learned in a step by step manner. It is the teacher's responsibility to make the students realize early on that it is up to them to do the work needed to advance. I tell my students that I want to assign enough homework so as to make the skill development an automatic process.

Because my students are either learning to drive, or have recently mastered the skills, it makes for a vivid comparison. I compare automaticity in learning algebra to learning to drive a car. At first, we notice every movement we make or plan to make when driving the car down a street. As we develop these skills, we reach down and turn on the radio or think about what we might do when we arrive at our destination. The actual skill of driving has become so automatic that we can let our minds go to other things. However, if a car pulls out in front of us, we can go back to the deliberate, conscious thinking of what driving skill we need to avoid an accident. If the students develop such automaticity in algebra, they become more and more able to advance at a desirable pace towards mastery of these skills.

I have yet another area of concern in my teaching of algebra. I feel that teacher-modeling is very necessary for the students to develop good habits in working algebra problems. "Thinking out loud" is a method I often employ. I put a problem on the overhead projector or the chalkboard. Then I act out the problem solving technique that I use in solving this problem. I actually say my thoughts as I go about working the problem and write the steps on the board. I even say the reason why I do a certain thing in a step of the problem. Then when I have the correct answer, along with checking, if possible, I turn the class time over to the students to ask questions or to offer alternate methods of working the same problem. Let's face it, there are numerous ways to work algebra problems. A teacher is short-sighted to demand that the students work a problem exactly as he/she would. Different brains process information differently, and different students will use different steps toward the solution of the same problem. I repeatedly tell my students that I want to teach many methods of working the same problem. Then, unless told to work the problem in a specific way, I allow them the freedom to choose the method they think is best.

For instance, in teaching the students to graph a line, I teach the arbitrary point method (called "choose-an-x; find-a-y" method), and then I teach the intercept method as a different way to accomplish the same task.

When testing this concept, I include problems specifying which method should be used as well as problems in which the students may choose the method that they feel is most appropriate for that particular solution.

I like to see students growing in other ways, too. In classwork or homework, I ask students to recognize the various methods of presenting their problem to me. The students may want to give me a visual message, for example: "Look at my working of the problem and tell me where I went wrong." For an alternative interaction, I sometimes insist that they give me an auditory message. I tell them to explain their work to me. Many times they realize their error just by doing this. I feel that it is good for them to learn to present messages in verbal form to a teacher. As the course progresses, I watch them getting better and better at doing this.

Questioning techniques are a big part of my teaching, too. I ask questions of all students, not just the volunteers. I give them time to think about the answer. If they experience difficulty in giving the answer, I give them a clue instead of going on to another student. I try to praise initiative on the part of any student who gives a partial answer or an erroneous answer. But I always clarify the correct answer for the student.

A teacher must learn to read from the expressions on the students' faces and determine when they understand or when they are confused. It is so gratifying to teach and explain a concept and to see students' faces turn on like lightbulbs, one at a time and different ones at different times. Actually, anything short of that means moving on to "plan B". It is not getting across to them. Another way I have of eliciting positive affective results is by the awarding of bonus points as a reward system. I award bonus points when least expected. For example, after encouraging the students to always use a pencil instead of pen when working math problems, I award five points to all students who do their work in pencil on a given day. It never fails that students do the following night's homework in pencil in hope of gaining those beloved bonus points. They never know when they may get rewarded and I keep it that way. However, I always include a bonus point problem on tests. The students seem to work harder and to be motivated to get those points. And, I get motivated by anything that turns them on.

The first step in maintaining a positive affective environment is to cultivate a healthy, but business-like student-teacher rapport. For example, one day after a student made the remark that algebra was too hard, I stated, "Algebra is your friend!" The other students got a good chuckle out of this. The next day I was emphasizing the fact that checking is crucial to determine if an answer is correct. The same student chimed in, "Checking is your friend, too. Isn't it, Mrs. Harper?" Surprisingly, the remark about algebra being one's friend kept popping up all semester. The idea spread to my other classes, from which came a real attention getter. When I made out the end of year examination, I purposefully did not include a bonus problem. I knew that the students would notice it. When the first class came in to take the test, I had explained all of the directions, and asked if there were any questions. One student asked where the bonus was. I said, "What Bonus?" Gasps could be heard throughout the room. The students said, "Mrs. Harper, you always give us a bonus." I told them for a bonus, if they desired the five bonus points, they could take one of two positions: 1) ALGEBRA IS MY FRIEND, or 2) ALGEBRA IS NOT MY FRIEND. They were to choose one and to explain the position they had taken.

Of the 147 students in five classes, only eight students took the negative position. The others gave various reasons that algebra was their friend. One student said that algebra was his friend because it made him feel so good when he got the problems right. That remark coins what I try to do in my algebra classes—to get maximum cognitive achievement while at the same time maintain a positive affective environment.

CHAPTER 25

AN ECLECTIC APPROACH
TO AFFECTIVE LEARNING

Dorothy M. Wesselmann

On a hot summer afternoon a seasoned teacher sits among the remnants of the past year. Decisions have to be made. Boxes of things must be examined, the contents of which are ideas used and discarded from the past years of teaching. Did the idea work? Is it worth trying again? Perhaps this one should have been presented differently. Each year brings another chance for the teacher to be more successful with the next group of students.

Contemplating a new school year barely a month away, the teacher has to ask once again the all important questions, "Why am I going back into the classroom?" After logically examining the assets and liabilities that lay in store for the year, automatically the answer comes. "I have a story to share and I have someone to share it with." Having satisfied the ego that the motive for returning to the classroom is a good one, the work continues.

Anxiety wells up again until an avalanche of questions overwhelms the consciousness. Why did Brian tell us that he was dropping out of school? He had had enough of school and in July he would be sixteen. Why do good kids like Brian get crushed in the very institution that is supposed to give them the necessary "stuff" to deal with the real world as they face the responsibilities of becoming an adult?

Are there more Brians ahead? Who are these people? What are their needs? Where did they come from? Do they know who they are? Do they care who they are? What can I teach them? Will I be able to reach out to them and find their needs? And, in finding their needs, can I be a facilitator of a useful learning experience?

These students come to the school year with all kinds of hope and fears. They have experienced successes and failures in their brief few years of life. They have been influenced by family backgrounds, community structures, peer groups, and the educational system. What will be the influence of this school year?

It is important to get to know the students as persons in order to really recognize their unique potentials. The students' special abilities as well as their special needs must surface before the teacher can really know them and plan for the special needs of each of them. The learning patterns are so different and varied from student to student. Therefore, there must be a lot of variation in the lesson preparations for the first couple of weeks of classes. Once the teacher gets to know the students, their needs become apparent. Recognizing their needs and preparing lesson plans which address their needs is a constant task for the rest of the year.

It is an accepted fact among many educators that teaching methods which stimulate the affective domain will more successfully reach the needs of all the students. As a science instructor in the middle school area, the most effective means for this teacher is to use large and small group activities for the first days of the school year. These types of activities are usually problem solving, brainstorming, challenging situations and shared experiences; because, they lend themselves most easily to teaching methods that can be used to involve the students towards the attainment of positive affective results.

Group activities provide freedom of expression for the individual student. This also gives the teacher time to become aware of personalities and attitudes as well as academic strengths and weaknesses as the students interact with each other. These group activities could be either teacher generated or student generated activities. And, they generally grow out of the flow of the subject matter being presented.

The teacher makes observations and evaluations of the groups and guides them towards the establishment of a code of conduct for the class. A plan of action and code of conduct are worked out that are acceptable to the students as well as the teacher. It includes expectations from both, the students and the teacher and usually includes rules of order, respect for each other, and calls for an acceptable amount of patience and listening to each other. Activity groups are formed, each devising a code of conduct for its members. These are written down on large sheets of paper and displayed. The code may need to be revised from time to time during the year. As a pattern of behavior and routine begins to emerge, broader topics for study can be suggested and the work divided among the groups, and finally among the members of the groups.

The group size is usually set by the teacher and may vary from class to class. However, the selection of those to be in each work group is done by the students, themselves. This is a delicate process and requires the patience of both students and teacher. The students will have to make some decisions and negotiate with each other. This can be a very important learning experience for the first few days of class. Using this kind of student initiated activity leaves the teacher free to concentrate on helping the few students who are shy or afraid of being rejected and displaced.

Lesson plans for the class group work are very important. The more concrete they are the better. The procedure should be carefully outlined into steps to be taken by the students all along the way. These steps need to be posted a few at a time at the proper time during the class. Doing this saves time and hassle for the students and the teacher. The activities that are assigned these groups should increase in complexity as the ability of the group to work together grows. There may be need for adjusting group size or changing members from one group to another from day to day to facilitate a smooth and orderly class. This will depend on the expertise of the teacher.

The curriculum guide for the school system will dictate WHAT must be studied and what should be mastered. The WHEN and HOW is left to the teacher's discretion to be organized in a meaningful way. Some teachers prefer to follow the trend of study set forth by a textbook that has been adopted for use by the school system. Other teachers prefer to go it on their own without following a textbook. These teachers often will select the material from the curriculum guide as it becomes relevant and of interest of the students.

It is important to build a file of ideas and interesting topics. The students are usually eager to help with this project because it means that they can make a contribution to the class that will be recognized and appreciated. A display area is also essential for this type of approach to the subject matter. The students usually have a lot of information and articles to share and every opportunity for them to share is important. When they bring things to share, there should be a place for these things to be put on display.

After the first couple of weeks have passed, what then? The heart of the school year begins in this eclectic setting. Group work may continue, whole class presentations may be given by the teacher in the form of demonstrations or lectures, or individual assignments may be performed. Whatever the method, a holistic approach must be used.

The following outline is suggested as an approach for organizing the class for an entire year (see Wesselmann, Chapter 20 in Sonnier, 1985a):

1. Decide on a topic from textbook or curriculum guide.

2. Brainstorm for ideas so as to subdivide and add to topic.

3. Define the scope. WHAT and HOW to present to class.

4. Select a workable vocabulary to grow as lesson unfolds.

5. Set a time schedule for research and presentations.

6. Select work groups as part of topic assignments.

7. Prepare the project or presentation. This is a time for individual and group research and material gathering.

8. Present the project to the class. Holistic and non-traditional methods are encouraged, e.g., hands-on, out-of-doors.

9. Evaluate the individual or group presentation by a scaler or oral evaluation by students and teacher, with emphasis on how to improve.

10. Formulate an evaluation of the topic for the class through objective and subjective as well as traditional and non-traditional means.

11. Evaluate the concepts learned by the entire class. Any and all of the above means can be and are used to evaluate academic achievement.

Careful planning, recognizing different student's needs and abilities, and using group activities are all important supplementary components of holistic teaching. By following the suggested outline, I have been able to implement holistic education while at the same time be in a better position to more adequately and satisfactorily reach and teach each student. And, through these activities, I am able to maintain a relatively high degree of academic achievement while at the same time maintain a positive affective environment.

CHAPTER 26

VISUALIZING THE HAMBURGER STAND: SELF-DIRECTED TEACHER AT WORK

Linda Kay

When we touch our students through both hemispheres, we increase their potentials for both cognitive achievement and affective attainment. When we guide them through an experience in a classroom, we have the opportunity to reinforce cognitive learning as well as increase sensitivity in the affective domain. For example, "here and now" situations may be simulated when students are taught to visualize their surroundings as an altered state: the House of Representatives, a court room, a battlefield, Nicaragua. Scenarios, mock elections, mock trials and case studies are all techniques used in my civics class to reinforce cognitive learning experiences. These techniques in affective education typically involve the visual, holistic right hemisphere, while at the same time enrich the cognitive learning of the left hemisphere. This is the way that real learning takes place, for a child's mind can go anywhere, with a little help.

The technique of transforming "there and then" into "here and now" scenarios is introduced to the students at the beginning of each term. The following activity symbolizes a "here and now" situation in which students can identify. A piece of 8½ x 11 paper is held up for them to see. Previously the paper was prepared by tearing off a corner, wrinkling it slightly, making a crease in it and then flattening it out again. As it is held up, the students are asked to look at it and to say a word or two about it. "Just tell what you see," I say. Typical responses are: "Torn piece of paper" . . ."missing corner" . . ."folded" . . ."pentagon" . . ."suspended" . . ."careless" . . ."turning" . . ."spoiled" . . ."messy" . . ."partial." After a few minutes of these expected responses, I challenge them with this thought: "Those of you who said something, try it on for size and see if it might not also be a description of yourself. And if you didn't speak, think of what you remember and try that on for size and see how it fits." The idea is that of all the reality that we see, we pick and choose according to our personal motives. If we are hungry, we see the hamburger stand and not the hardware store next to it. In order to enliven a class experience, an activity must be relevant, something brought into the here and now. To bring government and reality of life into a civics classroom is a challenge. My students write to Congressmen and Legislators about their feelings on matters that we have debated. When they get replies, they suddenly feel that there is actually someone "out there" who is responding to them. The realization of this fact opens them to the possiblity that government is a reality.

We use the Blue Book (Official Mississippi Statistical Register) for many activities, including looking up addresses of Congressmen and Legislators. They get to know what is in the Blue Book, how to find the information and to write to the Secretary of State to get their own Blue Book. This is a real and exciting experience for many of my students.

The Mississippi Cooperative Extension Service involved all of the ninth grades in the county in a County Youth Government Week each year. Student "county and city executives," everyone from the supervisors to sheriff and constables, were elected from the ninth grade classes. The elections were conducted in the same manner as real elections, with campaigns and speeches made and ballots (similar to real ballots) cast. The winners of the elections (eight or so from each school in the county) spent a day conducting business with their real counterpart in government.

One year a girl from our school was elected to the office of County Attorney. She was touring the jail with the real County Attorney when she noticed behind the bars a boy from her class at school! He had been arrested the night before for holding up a convenience store. She was as shocked as the boy behind bars at the encounter. This was a very real, vivid experience for her. The reality that a person can be on one or the other side of the law was made very clear. The fact that laws are broken and penalties are paid for breaking them became relevant. During another year, several students were present at a trial in which a man who had been sentenced to three 45 year terms broke down and wept. The fact that a man who had committed a crime, for which he had been found guilty, could at the same time be a feeling person who did not want to be put in jail was made very real. Their sorrow for the man was deeply felt and they had empathy with him.

A few minutes of silence at the beginning of a "here and now" lesson is a crucial leadership technique. I have learned that students hunger for structure, which allays their anxiety. Silence gives space for structure to be created out of any chaos that may exist and generates strong feelings among group members. Silence may be used throughout the group's life to provide space to present samples of the characteristic behavior patterns used in everyday situations. Silence is used further as a permissive tool, permitting a person to get up enough nerve to introduce something about himself. It permits shared interchanges to blossom fully and completely before moving on to the next order of business. Finally, silence may be used in culmination as a lack of closure experience. For example, someone may ask Lewis, "Were you having any feelings while Joan was talking?" Answer: "Yes". Silence. He is not closed off by words. He is allowed to feel and to express himself only if he chooses to do so.

After teaching a unit on the legislative branch of government, I have my students write their own bills. I show them copies of real bills from the Mississippi legislature as well as many bills written by students and presented at Youth Congress, which are usually shorter and of more interest to the high school students. The bills must be on a subject that could actually be dealt with by the legislature and something that they feel really needs to be enacted into law. After the bills have been "filed" at the "clerk's desk," the "Speaker" assigns bills to "committees" and the bills are debated. By this time, the students have sufficient experience role playing and have put so much of themselves into their bills, that the fervor with which authors present their bills to the class is amazing. They really feel crushed if a bill is defeated. They feel a personal loss if a "burning issue" does not catch everyone else on fire. Thus, they get a vivid experience in the process of how bills become law. Indeed, roles become so vivid that de-roling sometimes becomes a necessity. I do that by freezing their actions, retreating into silence, and returning to here-and-now reality. The conflict of values seen here is discussed after the de-roling has been accomplished. We discuss why some people are not into some issue and how this affects real legislation. For the last ten or fifteen minutes of class for several days we debate many of the students' bills. If necessary, bills are also debated at the beginning of class the next day. Students love to do this and many want to send good bills that they have passed in class on to the real legislature to try to get the idea into "real" law.

A decision tree may be used to introduce concepts of consequences, alternatives and goals in making decision. A scenario in which a student who has seen a friend cheating on a test is discussed and alternatives of action are written on one of the three "branches" of alternatives. Students usually mention alternative actions which might be taken, for instance, (1) talk to the friend after class, but let her cheat, (2) report the friend to the teacher during the test, or (3) do nothing at all. Then each alternative is discussed regarding both good and bad consequences in each situation. These are written on the decision tree in the appropriate places.

I remind students that sometimes it is easier to think of goals when they need to make a decision. For example, they might start at the top of the decision tree (the goal) by asking, "What do I want?" When they know their goals, the problem is to choose a good alternative to reach them. Sometimes, however, it may be easier to think of alternatives but harder to think of the goals. When this happens, they will probably start by asking, "What alternatives are there?" Thinking of alternatives helps them to think more clearly about their goals.

The decision tree is used many times in the civics course with case studies relating to the executive branch of government (how governors and others make decisions), the legislative branch (how lawmakers make decisions), and how citizens make decisions (as voters and tax payers). By starting with a personal incident, such as a friend cheating on a test, the students more readily understand the relevancy of looking at alternatives in any decision. It comes home to them in a real way and as they expand into more complex decisions and read about or role play the more abstract decisions, they are able to get into the models with little trouble. Other methods I use to implement holistic and affective education are aimed at exploring conflicts in which divisions are discouraged. These methods must encourage students by assuring them that they will gain something by cooperating, or lose by not cooperating. A method must encourage students to step out of social roles in their interactions, since social roles often have built-in conflicts, and if the student continues to act out these social roles, conflict will emerge.

During County Youth Government Week, four "parties" run a slate of officers—one party for each civics or history class. Each party writes its own platform, helps its candidates who have been elected within the class in a "primary" election, and try to get its party members elected. Competition is built between the classes. The classes discuss the competition. We discuss the value of having one's own class represented—the more representatives they get elected, the more class time will be spent in discussing the experiences of those who are elected to office (and the more "off task" time for the observers!). Students perceive winning as a valuable goal to work on as a group. What students consider "off-task" time, I consider "experiential learning." It is learning, but not out of the book, although students use the terms and ideas which they have just cognitively learned within the experiential learning situation.

Sometimes I have students fantasize about their families as they might be in the future. It is interesting to see what they think their town will be like when they are forty. It is very depressing to realize the number of students who believe that the world might not be here when they are forty. Through learning how to communicate with others in open honesty and trust, perhaps our students will be assured that there still will be a world in which they can visualize the hamburger stand and the hardware store when they are forty . . . and, when their children are forty.

PART VIII

VISUAL AFFECT AND ANALYTICAL AFFECT: THE DIFFERENT WORLDS THAT CREATE AND MOLD INDIVIDUAL DIFFERENCES

Saundra Y. McGuire, Editor

Visual learners and analytical learners experience vast differences in their educational encounters even though they may sit through the same classes. The visual learner sometimes finds that going to school means having to struggle through the abstractions and symbolisms of reading, writing, and arithmetic. On the other hand, the analytical learner often finds that school attendance means having to devise a creative poster or booklet cover—a task for which he/she has little or no aptitude. However, educational experiences do not have to be unpleasant for either the visual or the analytical learner if teachers really understood the characteristics of these two very different types of learners. In this section a visual person (Chapter 27) and an analytical person (Chapter 28) describe what it is like to be visual or analytical—the joys and frustrations as well as the events of acceptance and rejection. The major objective of this section is to explore the basis for providing all students with a greater degree of academic success and with the attendant positive affective results. In general, the assets of the visual learner, such as keen insight, creativity, and visual thinking skills, are the liabilities of the analytical learner who often shys away from tasks that require these skills. Furthermore, the liabilities of the visual learner, such as the as the inability to handle abstractions and to think symbolically, are the assets of the analytical learner. Since each type of learner has definite assets, the educational experience can and should be structured to emphasize these assets. Both visual and analytical learners have their academic ups and downs. Although unintentional and without malice, the DOWNS appear to be needlessly imposed by educators who are unaware of the significance that the differences in visual and analytical learners have on the affective results of the educational experience.

Social styles are yet another nature/nurture exhibition of individual differences that emerge from hemispheric preference (Chapter 29). A better understanding of the mutually exclusive traits of the two extremes, extremely visual and extremely analytical, helps one to come to grips with the array of these blended qualities in the majority of people who are eclectic individuals.

S. Y. McG.

CHAPTER 27

CHARACTERISTICS OF THE VISUAL PERSON

Isadore L. Sonnier

A visual person does not normally have difficulty intermeshing with home and community life. This individual difference is not easily observed in these environments. However, a number of problems systematically unfold throughout the life-long process of developing academic skills and becoming more analytical. This is especially true because of the expectations that are imposed during early childhood education. The academic demands of elementary education seem to start many of these individuals "off on the wrong foot," so to speak. Although according to traditional practice, there appears to be nothing wrong with demanding these skills, the nature and intensity of the demands are what we pass in review—the methods, not the motives.

Some learning environments seem to exaggerate several characteristics of the visual persons' individual differences. Visual learners appear to have in common a pronounced difficulty in learning in abstraction and with symbolisms. Both research and experience bear out as fact that reading, writing and arithmetic can only be successfully grasped when taught in a linear-logical manner using visual stimuli, and presented with careful, step-by-step, and thorough (linear-logical) explanations.

In that the necessity for this procedure MAY NOT have been clearly understood in the past, visual learners were categorized as slow learners and were systematically degraded and often needlessly separated from class groups. Further, these children were characterized with boredom, inattentiveness, day-dreaming, and other aberrant behaviors that may have been misconstrued to warrant taking disciplinary action. Mismanaged lesson planning is at the heart of this scenario. Typically, the materials may not have been presented in a step-by-step, linear-logical manner. The pace may have been too fast, or, there may have been excessive dependency on verbal communications, any of which would have resulted in compounding the level of difficulty for these learners. Perhaps more from experience than from existing research, it is suggested that visual students can be schooled into sound linear-logical thinking, just as linear-logical students can be schooled into sound and effective visual thinking. Much research is needed in this area. However, if it is true that these propensities can be schooled, then HOLISTIC EDUCATION is offered as a monumental solution to the entire problem. For indeed, holistic educational strategies reach both propensities simultaneously and concurrently with exactly that purpose in mind—to make visual students more efficient in linear-logical thinking and linear-logical students more effective with visual mentations.

A passing remark MUST be made about testing procedures. I was reminded of this recently when a straight, uninterrupted hour of complicated calculations left me with different answers to a simple addition column, three times in a row—nothing a ten-minute break couldn't cure. *Analytical thought processing is tiring and fatiguing for visual persons.* I was reminded and herein point out that long tests have always left me *physically* and *mentally* depleted—often a test of alert endurance with attrition and erosion of analytical effectiveness. Marathon tests may well discriminate against visual persons because of fatigue, thereby inhibiting aptitude.

With that introduction, I will discuss what it is like to be a visual person using my own background of experiences. I remember mostly the loving teachers that molded these experiences. True to form and characteristic, I did not learn to read until the fifth grade or so, when for reasons and circumstances I can't remember, I started going over books that had been read to me in earlier years, many in our own family library (which means that having books around did not help up to this point, reflecting on the importance of the environment. However, they were Godsent when needed). I knew the stories by heart (the heart is often substituted for the mind—

particularly the right hemisphere—here, it is the seat of long-term memory).
I can remember the written words taking on new meaning. However, it
must also be told as part of this story that I have never been able to read
orally with any degree of competence. Even with years of practice, mostly
practice done in skimming over the text of a page with a moderately high
degree of comprehension, oral reading is still a disaster. For, some words
are picked up out of sequence and out come these wrong words when least
expected—a classic case of dyslexia. I needed help earlier-on that my loving
teachers did not know how to provide. Few of them probably even suspected that I needed help. Mathematics education is a source of difficulty
for visual students at all levels of learning. I choose to describe two statistics classes as typical and characteristic of the life-long experience in this
area. The two teachers that I describe could personify any teacher in primary
or secondary education. They are identified as Teacher A and Teacher B.

Teacher A walked into the room the first day of class. Silently and deliberately, he fingered each individual in a pointing jesture as he counted the
30 or so of us present. Still silent, he turned to the chalkboard and performed a formulated calculation, turned around and announced that seven
of us would fail this course. I was at the time teaching his seventh grade
son who was struggling in my science class (as he was in all of his classes).
The C that I made in this statistics class was probably more of a political
favor than a reflection of the skills that I could demonstrate on tests.
However, as is characteristic of visual learners, I learned more than could
be demonstrated on tests.

My second statistics course was with a lady who had taught upper elementary and junior high school students for years and was still teaching at that
level—even to graduate students. Teacher B always assumed that we came
into the course with little or no previous understanding of each topic that
she taught us. I performed much more effectively in this class—for this
teacher. I got a lot more out of this course than I did in my first course.
More importantly, I enjoyed and savored each moment of it and still pride
myself in the application of statistical treatments learned in that course.

Therein seems to lie the answer to many of these thorny questions about
what makes one course more affectively influential than another. It is always the teacher. It can only be the teacher. It can never be anything more
nor less than the teacher. And, the only logic that I can place on the process

is that of *communications*. The effective teacher communicates—teaches. The ineffective teacher fails to communicate and leaves too many unanswered questions in the minds of learners. Step-by-step communication, with visual aids. . . HOLISTIC STRATEGIES beget NOT ONLY a higher degree of achievement, they beget affective results! (See Chapters 17 and 18).

These two teachers and strategies were selected with the purpose of discussing which of these teachers was visually oriented and which was linear-logical. Although more from experience than from research, either could have been visual or analytical. Teacher A behaved much like an analytical person, using traditional/authoritarian teaching strategies, as indicated by so much concern for the content taught. However, in that this form of teaching is rather exclusively the only model available to imitate, it is common for a visual person to use this mode, rather than the self-directed mode for which they are better philosophically suited. Teacher A could have been either a visual or an analytical person. Teacher B behaved much like a visual person, practicing self-directed methods, demonstrated in the concern for students. However, analytical persons are NOT BEYOND concern for students in such a loving and caring manner. She could have been either visual or analytical. Experience tells me, concerning this parameter, that the end product of good teaching is the same NO MATTER WHICH—visual or analytical. Though philosophies differ, the results are the same (I cite 15 years of experience with many informal observations—while awaiting further research).

The conclusion concerning students and teachers is that visual students appear to do well in project and task-oriented learning environments. Again, drawing from my experiences as a student in the U.S. Marine Corps in radio operating and repairing classes, learning side by side with analytical students (and probably some well schooled visual persons), I remember how easily it all came for these friends and how from time to time, though on rare occasion, I "saw" an idea with apparently more "insight." These classes were conducted in the effective manner as described by D. Sonnier for holistic learning as a key to military training (see Chapter 14).

CHAPTER 28

CHARACTERISTICS OF THE
ANALYTICAL PERSON

Saundra Y. McGuire

As is the case with the visual person, the analytical person does not normally have difficulty in home life. In fact, it is quite likely that either one or both parents and some siblings are also analytically rather than visually oriented. Unlike the visual person, the analytical person generally experiences a fair amount of success in school because subjects such as reading, writing, and arithmetic place a great deal of emphasis on analytical thinking skills. However, there are weaknesses in the analytical person that could put the person at odds with the academic environment. When teachers are aware of this, they can employ holistic educational strategies to put the analytical learner back in "sync." In this chapter we will explore the questions of what an analytical person is, how one gets to be an analytical person, the strengths and weaknesses of the analytical learner, and the holistic educational strategies that strengthen analytical learners.

What Is an Analytical Person? An analytical person is one who usually considers the details of a situation rather than the integrated picture. These persons are very good at following instructions and in processing information in a linear-logical fashion. Processing symbolic information generally poses no problem for the analytical person because it is easy for him/her to mentally keep track of what each symbol represents. For this reason, these individuals are usually quite good at reading, writing, and mathematics in school. These subjects, as taught in most schools, require students to associate individual letters with individual sounds, to memorize sets of rules, and to use abstract logic. As reported by Sonnier (Chapter 27) the visual person has difficulty learning in abstractions and with symbols. The analytical person, on the other hand, thrives on these types of tasks and is actually made to feel "more intelligent" than peers who are visual persons instead of analytical. The nemesis for the analytical person, however, is open-ended projects that have no well-defined set of instructions. I can still remember quite well the feelings of total inadequacy I experienced when faced with the second grade task of designing a book cover for a book all about myself and my family. I watched in frustration as my visually oriented classmates happily went about the task of designing creative and aesthetically pleasing book covers without the least bit of difficulty. And the teacher's comments concerning my inability to perform this simple task when I was such a "good student" certainly did not help my affect at the time. Although I did not realize it at the time, this was probably my first real experience with the idea that analytical as well as visual learners can have very unpleasant learning experiences if teachers are unaware of the learning style of students and are not in tune with the affective needs of students.

How Does One Get to Be An Analytical Person? The question of what causes a person to be an analytical or a visual person has not been fully answered. Although there are educational theorists who propose that these characteristics are fixed from birth, most educators are of the opinion that one's experiences determine the type of learning style with which one is most comfortable. Hence, the familiar nature vs. nurture question arises again. I am of the conviction that it is indeed one's early childhood *environment* that determines whether an individual will be primarily visual or primarily analytical in the approach to learning. When one considers the hemisphericity model in which the linear-logical, analytical tasks are a function of left-brain information processing and the visuo-spatial, holistic tasks are a function of the right-brain, the question of the development of an information-processing style is still not definitively answered. Some studies have attempted to show that newborn babies exhibit cerebral dominance. However, other studies have demonstrated a distinct link between culture and hemisphericity. For example, studies performed with Oriental students raised in an Eastern culture indicate that they are more right-hemisphere dominant in thought processes than are Westerners. Additionally, cross cultural studies using Black and White students have indicated that Black students are more likely to prefer right-hemisphere educational tasks such as writing creative stories. Hence, although there may be a genetically determined component to learning style, preferences appear to be largely environmentally determined.

When attempting to relive experiences from my childhood while trying to determine how I developed into an analytical person, I recalled many instances during which my father, who was a science teacher, would pose mathematical brain-teasers which required that I employ some type of mathematical formula. Additionally, my mother, who was an elementary teacher, stressed reading skills and learning to speak with precise grammar. Between the two of them, my focus on correct rules and symbolism and following directions was firmly grounded in my thinking style. There was little room for creativity in my childhood. Everything was very precise.

Thus, to answer the question, "How does one get to be an analytical person," I must say "The same way one gets to be a visual person – through experiences that tend to reinforce one style of thinking over another." As we now know, there are benefits and deficiencies inherent in both styles and neither is a priori superior to the other. The affective climate would improve for all students if teachers would emphasize the strengths of both styles in a holistic teaching style that brings them both into focus.

Strengths of the Analytical Person. Because of the emphasis on linear-logical, analytical thought in the Western culture, analytical individuals appear to have the advantage. The strengths of the analytical person become evident as soon as the child enters school. Reading and writing and arithmetic are often favorite subjects and the pupil seems to perform these tasks effortlessly. The ability to categorize information into neat little packets in the brain comes in quite handy when the correct spelling of a word must be recalled or the correct mathematical formula must be employed. This is what the analytical person does best – quantify and analyze individual bits of information for easy recall when necessary. Remembering and following directions also seems to come quite easily to the analytical person.

After all, rules are linear-logical by nature. Any and all subjects that lend themselves well to rules, formulas, or equations are strengths of the analytical person.

Weaknesses of the Analytical Person. Although the weaknesses of a person who is decidedly analytical in thinking style may not be as obvious in the American learning environment as those of a student who is decidedly visual, individuals who rely almost solely on analytical thought processes do indeed have many weaknesses. Probably one of the most serious weaknesses is the inability to look at issues and topics from a global perspective. The analytical person is locked into considering bits and pieces of a subject rather than the whole. Because of this many analytical students are not very successful at concept attainment. They are quite good at memorizing all of the individual pieces of a concept, but invariably fail to see how the pieces fit together to produce a whole concept. These students are the students who, when faced with any type of word or "story" problem, will immediately ask "What formula do I need to use?" They constantly seek to pigeonhole any and every bit of information into a certain type. However, when faced with an open-ended problem that they are unable to categorize into a known type, the analytical student becomes frustrated. At that point the learning environment becomes uncomfortable and the affective results are negative.

Holistic Educational Strategies that Strengthen Analytical Learners. Now that we have a profile of the analytical person and we have seen both the strengths and weakness of visual and analytical individuals, we turn our attention to what types of teaching strategies can be used to strengthen the learning skills of the analytical learner.

The first teaching tool is *communication*. I am in total agreement with Sonnier (Chapter 27) when he states that "The effective teacher communicates — teaches." Although analytical learners are usually very successful students and are often categorized as gifted, being in a classroom in which the teacher fails to communicate expectations, goals, rules and regulations, and boundaries is an affective disaster for the analytical student. This type of student, moreso than the visual student, needs communication.

The second teaching tool is the ability and willingness to present the course material in a variety of formats in order to reach both the visual and the analytical learner. Demonstrating visual analogies to analytical problems is very useful to the student who has no inclination toward anything visual. After forming mental pictures an analytical thinker is better able to obtain a holistic view of a situation rather than of individual components to the whole.

The third and most important teaching tool is compassion for the learner — the ability to understand the problems associated with being an analytical person and the interest to help the student broaden his or her way of approaching subjects. For in the final analysis, a successful and affectively positive learning experience requires that students exhibit flexibility in their approach to learning and problem solving. The more analytical skills a visual learner acquires and the more visual skills an analytical learner acquires, the better and more efficient learner each will become. And after a while, as Sonnier has stated (Chapter 27), one will hardly be able to tell the difference between visual and analytical learners. This is the ideal toward which all teachers need to strive.

CHAPTER 29

SOCIAL STYLE AND THE HEMISPHERICITY MODEL

Isadore L. Sonnier

An attempt has been made to establish relationships between social style, teaching style, and learning style because of the outstanding assumption that they are all hemisphericity-based. This assumption has provided the motivation to make these plausible comparisons (see Chapter 15). Sonnier shares some of the findings of the research on social style and offers suggestions for further research. This contribution is intended to present the educational community with yet another area of individual differences in need of assimilation and incorporation towards the better understanding of neuroeducation.

S.Y.McG.

The Social Style Profile was developed by Wilson Learning Corporation for the purpose of improving the quality of one's interpersonal relationships, a service that has been particularly helpful for individuals in the business community. A person's social style is defined in terms of *assertiveness and responsiveness*, with *versatility* as an interwoven factor in both of these

---

These discussions are abstracted from Lashbrook, V.J. and Lashbrook, W.B. (1980). "Social Style as a basis for adult training," Presented to Central States Speech Association, Communication Theory Division, Chicago, IL. For further information on social style, contact Wilson Learning Corporation, Eden Prairie, MN, 55344.

parameters. According to Lashbrook and Lashbrook (1980), norms were established and for the purpose of simplification, four of the emerging styles are discussed. Those styles are: ANALYTICAL (lowly assertive and lowly responsive), AMIABLE (lowly assertive and highly responsive), DRIVER (highly assertive and lowly responsive), and EXPRESSIVE (highly assertive and highly responsive). ASSERTIVENESS is that expression of one's attempt to control or influence others, easily detected as a task-oriented dimension of one's social style. Assertive individuals make every attempt to be active, confident, aggressive, ambitious, challenging, competitive, fast-paced, risk-taking, opinionated, and directive. LOW ASSERTIVENESS, on the other hand, means to be reserved, easy going, submissive, private, quiet, supportive, cooperative, deliberate, risk-avoiding, and unaggressive. Highly assertive persons are more frequently expressive communicators and are less apprehensive than those with low assertiveness.

RESPONSIVENESS is associated with one's emotional expressiveness and friendliness. It is considered to be a relationship-oriented dimension of one's social style. Highly responsive individuals are characterized as warm, approachable, people-oriented, emotional, permissive, subjective, easy going, open, sociable, and dramatic. Lowly responsive persons are described as being cool, independent, aloof, rational, objective, impersonal, cautious, and business-like. Highly responsive persons are less dogmatic and less apprehensive than lowly responsive individuals and are, therefore, more apt to excel, or at least succeed, in social encounters and relationship establishments.

VERSATILITY refers to a person's ability to adapt to other styles and various interpersonal situations, a dimension that cuts through all of the other parameters and mediates in the effectiveness of one's social style. Although each person usually behaves in a manner consistent with his or her social style, one's versatility is the degree to which temporary modifications can be made so as to become compatible with others' styles. Highly versatile individuals are generalists, adaptable, tolerant of ambiguity, negotiable, flexible, and multidimensional in their thinking. Lowly versatile persons, on the other hand, are more than likely to be specialists, single minded, predictable, intolerant of ambiguity, and inflexible.

THE FOUR SOCIAL STYLES, based on these parameters are: ANALYTICALS, often described as technical specialists. They are industrious, persistent, serious, vigilant, orderly, uncommunicative, indecisive, stuffy, exacting, and impersonal. Since they are low in both assertiveness and responsiveness, they tend to make limited use of personal power and emotional expression.

AMIABLES, who are low in assertiveness but high in responsiveness, are characteristically supportive specialists; dependable, respectful, personable, conforming, retiring, non-commital, undisciplined, and emotional. While they tend to hold their personal power in check, they freely express themselves emotionally.

DRIVERS can be thought of as control specialists since they are highly assertive, but lowly responsive. They tend to use their personal power, while controlling the expressions of their emotion. They are characterized as determined, thorough, decisive, efficient, pushy, tough-minded, dominating, and harsh.

EXPRESSIVES are considered to be social specialists due to the high degree of their assertiveness and responsiveness. They also tend to freely express emotions and make use of their personal powers. They tend to be personable, stimulating, enthusiastic, dramatic, inspiring, opinionated, promotional, undisciplined, and excitable.

AN OUTSTANDING CONCLUSION that can be drawn from these findings is that social styles could be the nature-nurture expressions of the hemisphericity phenomenon. In support of this conclusion, ANALYTICALS display almost exclusively, the propensities of the analytical hemisphere with apparently little, if any, input from the visual hemisphere. On the other hand, EXPRESSIVES display almost exclusively, the propensities of the visual hemisphere with apparently little analytical input. However, AMIABLES and DRIVERS display blended qualities of these two hemispheric propensities. In that the analytical hemisphere (left in most people) is the seat of linear-logical, abstract thinking, it is in all probability the dominant force in the behavior of DRIVERS. The visual hemisphere (right in most people) is the seat of holistic, configurational thinking, but more important, it is the seat of human emotions. Thus, the visual hemisphere is in all probability the dominant force in the behavior of AMIABLES.

While these are relatively uncorroborated conclusions, they are offered for further investigation with confidence that IF the relationships are not precisely as suggested, they are most certainly a step in the right direcion. The administration and discussion of the *Hemispheric Preference Inventory*, which includes four items on social styles (adapted from Ingrasci, 1981, p. 62) are herein presented in Chapter 15 (see also Figure 18.1, p. 140).

PART IX
TOPICS IN NEED OF FURTHER STUDY

Isadore L. Sonnier, Editor

A primary objective of this project was to make a case for hemisphericity as a basis for individual differences, holistic education, and helping students to attain positive affective results. A list of topics in need of further study comes to mind in these early revelations of hemisphericity and neuroeducation. However, they are but a ripple on the still and deep waters of the educational enterprise, offered as an invitation for others to continue these investigations.

I.L.S.

CHAPTER 30

TOPICS IN NEED OF FURTHER STUDY

Isadore L. Sonnier, Editor

Rex Leonard

1. Monitoring the results of neuroeducation, learning styles, and methods and techniques of holistic education.

2. Conducting longitudinal studies of neuroeducation, learning styles, and methods and techniques of holistic education.

3. Conducting action research to establish the parameters of neuroeducation as they now stand in the public schools.

4. Research in instrument development to clarify the paradigms of creativity-conductivity and the visualizing-analyzing methods of consciousness.

5. Replication studies to enhance refinement of prospective instruments in addition to solidifying the theoretical bases on which hemisphericity models currently rest.

6. Conducting longitudinal studies of hemispheric preference to determine if within an individual it remains constant over time.

7. Research to determine the implications of hemisphericity on teacher preparation.

Patty M. Ward

1. To what extent does curriculum today address affective education?

2. To what extent do teachers educate for affective results?

3. Pre- and post-tests to ascertain affective results of neuroeducational strategies.

4. What strategies are most effective with visual learners?

5. What strategies are most effective with analytical learners?

6. What materials are most effective with the different learners?

7. To what extent do schools attempt to involve parents of minority students?

Tressie S. Harper

1. Hemisphericity and Advanced Mathematics. To what extent is hemisphericity a factor in the learning of algebra and plane geometry? Should the sequencing of these courses take these hemispheric considerations into account?.

2. To what extent is hemisphericity, visual and analytical, involved in the selection and use of audio-visual equipment?

3. To what extent are visual and analytical learners affected by various physical learning environments, (for example, the many lighting systems)?

Lisardo Doval Salgado

1. Further research is needed to determine those neuropsychological parameters that are basic to teaching and learning styles.

2. Diagnosis of thinking-learning styles and teaching-learning modes so as to more adequately structure teacher-education curricula.

3. Further research is needed on cerebral hemisphericity as it applies to curriculum development.

4. Further research is needed to determine those educational goals and objectives that meet the different hemispheric preference needs.

5. Operational definitions are needed for self-directed and authoritarian modes of teaching.

Miguel A. Santos Rego

1. Research is needed to better understand the different teaching styles and ways to evaluate the ways that each contribute to learning in the classroom.

2. Research is needed to determine better ways to bring a higher level of academic success for poor and non-achievers.

3. Ways are needed to holistically teach problem solving strategies to all of the different learning styles.

4. Research is needed to determine if more emphasis should be paid at the university level on how teaching-learning styles can better serve the different cognitive styles so as to bring academic success to more students.

5. Research is needed to determine how teachers can bring about academic success for individual with different hemispheric preference.

Renato A. Schibeci

1. What kinds of attitudes are students acquiring that are relative to curricular objectives?

2. Are these attitudes acquired mainly inside or outside the classroom?

3. What classroom process variables are most closely linked with students' attitudes?

Luis M. Sobrado Fernandez

1. The development of teacher evaluation techniques are needed to identify those teaching skills that lead more learners to greater achievement.

2. The development of evaluation techniques are needed to determine the level at which a teacher education program is successfully implemented by teachers.

3. A study of the relationships between one's teaching style and the deci-

sion making techniques that one uses in the classroom is needed.

4. Further research is needed to determine if the more elaborate a lesson plan is, the more adequately it will meet the teacher's moment to moment needs.

Isadore L. Sonnier

1. Is the multiple tracking of students coherent with hemisphericity and holistic education?

2. To what extent can a comedian's cognitive and positive affective influence on the mass' attention be compared with holistic education, the reaching and teaching of both hemispheres simultaneously and concurrently?

3. To what extent can educators help visual persons to become more analytical and analytical persons to become more visual?

4. How can teacher educators alter the present curriculum so as to implement holistic education as a norm?

5. What are the ramifications of switched visual and analytical hemispheres in some humans? To what extent does this anomaly exist?

GLOSSARY

Affective Domain

That quality of learning dealing with feeling, attitudes, and often expressed in pleasure of learning.

Affective Education

The quality of learning as provoked and displayed in active, debative, and judgemental student dialogue, involving feelings, attitudes and pleasure of learning.

Affective State

In the learning environment, students are individually and collectively involved positively, neutrally, or negatively with the subject and the teacher.

Analytical Learners

Students who rely upon the propensities of the analytical cerebral processes of thinking and learning, often inappropriately called auditory learners.

Authoritarian Teaching

Teaching activities of the preferred mode for analytical individuals. Teacher-directed activities is the norm.

Cognitive Domain

The quantity learned, dealing with academic achievement.

213

Cognitive Education	The quality learned as provoked by the mental processing of information with reference to instructional efficiency and can be measured by criterion referenced test items.
Constructive Cognition	The mental processing skills of linear-logical, analytical individuals.
Creative Cognition	The mental processing technique and skills of visual individuals.
Eclectic Cognition	The mental processing skills of those individuals who possess and orchestrate both visual and analytical propensities.
Eclectic Teaching	Teaching activities of the vast majority of teachers, blending authoritarian and self-directed teaching activities. However, there is usually the display of one or the other as a preferred mode of teaching.
Hemisphericity	Humans display one or the other, but mostly both of the processes of visualizing and analyzing in their thinking, learning, social, teaching, and leadership styles, among others. Each is a dichotomous expression of the mutually exclusive propensities of the two hemispheres.
Holistic Education	The simultaneous and concurrent reaching and teaching of the two cerebral hemispheric processes through well sequenced visual aids and thorough explanations.
Holistic Instruction	See Holistic Education.
Leadership Styles	As displayed in the classroom in educational management, self-directed, eclectic and authoritarian, as a function of hemispheric preference/dominance.

Learning Styles	The mode of knowledge acquisition, a function of hemispheric preference/dominance, which includes visual, eclectic, and analytical processing.
Metacognitive Development	Student awareness of knowledge acquisition.
Neuroeducation	The recognition of holistic education, metacognitive development and other aspects of learning as functions of hemispheric preference/dominance. Also, hemisphericity based educational management confluent with hemisphericity based accountability.
Quality Learned	The degree to which students internalize the educational objectives in active, debative, judgemental discussion, as determined by the level of affective attainment.
Quantity Learned	The cognitive achievement or the amount of educational objectives learned or internalized through the efforts of a given teaching strategy, as measured by criterion referenced test items.
Self-Directed Teaching	Teaching activities of the prefered mode for visual individuals. Student-prompted activities are the norm.
Social Styles	The mode of social behavior, aside from those acquired, a function of hemispheric preference/dominance, including, analyticals, amiables, drivers, and expressives.
Teaching Styles	The mode of teaching preference, a function of hemispheric preference/dominance, including self-directed, eclectic and authoritarian.

Thinking Styles   The mode of thinking, a function of hemispheric preference/dominance, including visual, eclectic and analytical.

Visual Learners   Students that rely upon the propensities of visual cerebral processes in thinking and learning.

BIBLIOGRAPHY

Adler, P. (1975). "The transnational experience: an alternative view of culture shock," *Journal of Humanistic Psychology.* 15:13-23.

Alexander, W. M. (Ed.). (1967). *The changing secondary school curriculum: readings.* New York: Holt, Rinehart and Winston.

Amonker, R.G. (1980). "What do teens know about the facts of life?" *Journal of School Health.* 50:527-530.

Ausubel, D.P. (1968). *Educational psychology: a cognitive view.* New York: Holt, Rinehart and Winston.

Bain, L. (1980). "Socialization into the role of participant: physical education's ultimate goal," *Journal of Physical Education.* 51:48-50.

Beatty, W.E. (Ed.). (1969). *Improving educational assessment & an inventory of measures of affective behavior.* Washington, D.C.: Association for Supervision and Curriculum Development.

Bignell, S. (1982). *Sex education: Teacher's guide and resource manual.* Santa Cruz, California: Network Publications.

Bloom, B.S. (Ed.). (1956). *Taxonomy of educational objectives: the classification of educational goals, handbook I: cognitive domain.* New York: David McKay Company, Inc.

Bogen, J.E., DeZure, R., TenHouten, W.D., & Marsh, J.F. (l972). "The other side of the brain, IV: the A/P ratio,"*Bulletin of the Los Angeles Neurological Society*. 37:49-61.

Bogen, J.E. (1975). "Educational aspects of hemispheric specialization," *UCLA Educator*. 17:24-32.

_____. (1977). "Some educational implications of hemispheric specialization." In M.C. Wittrock. (Ed.). *The human brain* (pp. 133-152). Englewood Cliffs, NJ: Prentice-Hall.

Brislin, R.W. (1981). *Cross-cultural encounters* (pp. 155-163). Elmsford, N.Y.: Pergamon Press.

Bryant, W.H. (1984). "Assuming a French identity: The Affective Domain," *French Review*. 57:677-785.

Campbell, L.P. (1974). "Cognitive and affective: a dual emphasis," *Contemporary Education*. 46:13-14.

Carlson, J.B. (1981). "Fathoming feelings in physical education," *Journal of Physical Education and Recreation*. 52:19-21,54.

Carretero, M. y Palacios, J. (1982a). "Los estilos cognitivos. Introduccion al problema de las diferencias cognitivas individuales". *Infancia y Aprendizaje*, 1:20-28.

Carretero, M. y Palacios, J. (1982b). "Implicaciones educativas de los estilos cognitivos". *Infancia y Aprendizaje*. 2:83-106.

Di Vesta, F.J. & Finke, F.M. (1985). "Metacognition, elaboration, and knowledge acquisition," *Educational Communication and Technology Journal* 33:285-293.

Dodds, P. (1976). "Love and joy in the gymnasium," *Quest*. 26:109-116.

Dodds, P. & Locke, L.F. (1984). "Is physical education in American schools worth saving? Evidence, alternatives, judgement," (pp. 76-90). College Park, MD: *National Association of Physical Educators and Health Educators Proceedings*.

Dressel, P.L. (1976). *Handbook of Academic Evaluation*. San Francisco: Jossey-Bass.

Dunn, R., Cavanaugh, D.P., Eberle, B.M., & Zenhausern, R. (1982). "Hemispheric preference: the newest element of learning styles," *Journal of the National Association of Biology Teacher*. 44:291-294.

Edwards, B. (1979). *Drawing on the right side of the brain*. Los Angeles, CA 90069: J. P. Tarcher, Inc.

Entwistle, N. (1981). *Styles of learning and teaching*. New York: John Wiley and Sons.

Fiedler, F.E., Mitchell, T.R., & Triandis, H.D. (1971). "The culture assimilator: an approach to cross-cultural training," *Journal of Applied Psychology*. 55:95-102.

Frye, P. (1983). "Measurement of psychosocial aspects of physical education," *Journal of Physical Education, Recreation, and Dance*. 54:26-27.

Gallup, A. (1985), "The Gallup Poll of teachers' attitudes toward the public schools: Part 2." *Phi Delta Kappan*, 66:323-330.

Garanderie, A. de la (1983). *Los perfiles pedagogicos: descubrir las aptitudes escolares*. Madrid: Narcea.

Garber, E. (1926). Quoted in *A digest of investigations in the teaching of science* (p. 64), by F. D. Curtis. Philadelphia, PA: P. Blakison's Sons & Co.

Gazzaniga, M.S. (1975). "Review of the split brain," *UCLA Educator*. 17:9-12.

———. (1977). "Review of the split brain," In M.C. Wittrock. (Ed.). *The human brain* (pp. 89-96). Englewood Cliffs, NJ: Prentice Hall.

Gordon, S., Scales, P., & Everly, K. (1979). The sexual adolescent: communicating with teenagers about sex. Scituate, MA: Duxbury Press.

Gordon, S. (1981). "New Jersey's controversial mandate on family life education," *Phi Delta Kappan*. 63: 194-218.

Graham, G. & Heimerer, E. (1981). "Research on teacher effectiveness: a summary with implications for teaching," *Quest*. 33:14-25.

Griffin, P.S. (1983). "Second thoughts on affective evaluation," *Journal of Physical Education, Recreation, and Dance*. 52:25,86.

Griffin, P.S. (1983). "Gymnastics is a girl's thing: student participation and interaction patterns in a middle school gymnastic unit." In Templin, T.J. & Olson, J.K. (Eds.). *Teaching in physical education*. Champaign, IL: Human Kinetics Publishers.

Harrow, A.J. (1972). *A taxonomy of the psychomotor domain: a guide for developing behavioral objectives*. New York: David McKay.

Hassard, J. (1985). "Holistic teaching (from a humanistic view)." In I.L. Sonnier, (Ed.). *Methods and techniques of holistic education* (pp. 51-58). Springfield, IL: Charles C. Thomas, Publisher.

Health, Education, and Welfare Department. (1970). *Environmental education: education that cannot wait* (p. 38). Washington, D.C.: U. S. Office of Education.

Hellison, D. (1973). *Humanistic physical education*. Englewood Cliffs, NJ: Prentice-Hall.

Hellison, D. (1978). *Beyond ball and bats*. Washington, D.C.: American Alliance on Health, Physical Education, Recreation, and Dance.

Hillison, D. (1985). *Goals and strategies for teaching physical education*. In Templin, T.J. & Olson, J.K. (Eds.). *Teaching physical education*. Champaign, IL: Human Kinetics Publishers.

Hendrixson, L.L. (1981). "The case for a moral sex education in the schools," *Phi Delta Kappan*. 63:194-195.

Hispanics in HDS Programs. (1980). *A needs and services delivery assessment preliminary findings*, July 1980. Washington, D.C.: U. S. Department of Health and Human Services, Office of Human Development Services.

Hogan and Hartson. (1978). Letter dated November 21, 1978 to the Honorable Joseph A. Califano, Secretary of Health, Education and Welfare, Washington, D. C.

Ingrasci, H.J. (1981). "How to reach buyers in their psychological 'comfort zones,'" *Industrial Marketing*. 66:60-64.

Jorgensen, S.R. (1981). "Sex education and the reduction of adolescent pregnancies: Prospects for the 1980s." *Journal of Early Adolescence*. 1:38-52.

Kagan, J., Rosman, B.L., Day, D., Albert, J., & Phillips, W. (1983). "Information processing in the child: significance of analytic and reflective attitudes," *Psychological Monographs*. 78:No. 578, 1964, 37pp.

Keefe, J.W. (Ed.). (1982). *Student learning styles and brain behavior*. Reston, VA: National Association of Secondary School Principals.

Keogh, J. & Sugden, D. (1985). *Motor skill development*. New York: McMillan.

Kerr, R. (1982). *Psychomotor learning*. Philadelphia: Saunders.

Kirby, D., Alter, J., & Scales, P. (1979). *An analysis of U. S. sex education programs and evaluation methods*. Springfield, VA: National Technical Information Service.

Kogan, N. (1981). "Las implicaciones de los estilos cognoscitivos en la educacion." En G.S. Lesser, (Ed.). *La psicologia en la practica educativa* (303-366). Mexico: Trillas.

Kohlberg, L. (Ed.). (1973). *Collected papers on moral development and moral education*. Cambridge, MA: Harvard University, Laboratory for Human Development.

Kohler, W. (1966). *The place of value in a world of facts*. New York: Mentor Books, New American Library, Inc., p. x.

Kollen, P.P. (1983). "Fragmentation and integration in human movement." In Templin, T.J. & Olson, J.K. (Eds.). *Teaching physical education*. Champaign, IL: Human Kinetics Publishers.

Krashen, S.D. (1975). "The left brain," *UCLA Educator*. 17:17-23.

Krathwohl, D.R., Bloom, B.S., & Masia, B.B. (1964). *Taxonomy of educational objectives: handbook II, the affective domain*. New York: David McKay Co.

Landis, D., Day, H.R., McGrow, P.L., Thomas, J.A., & Miller, A.B. (1976). "Can a black 'culture assimilator' increase racial understanding?" *Journal of Social Issues*. 32:169-183.

Lashbrook, V.J. & Lashbrook, W.B. (1980). "Social styles as a basis for adult training." Presented to Central States Speech Association, Communication Theory Division, Chicago, IL. (Eden Prairie, MN, 55344: Wilson Learning Corporation).

Leonard, R. & Boulter, W.F. (1985). "Developing an instrument to measure the modes of consciousness in humans." In I.L. Sonnier, (Ed.). *Methods and techniques of holistic education* (pp. 72-79). Springfield, IL: Charles C. Thomas, Publisher.

Litwach, L., Linc, L., & Bower, D. (1985). *Evaluation in nursing: principles and practice*. New York: National League for Nursing.

Lynch, J.J. (1981). "Humanistic education in secondary school—facts and fantasies," *NASSP Bulletin*. 65:82-87.

Mackenzie, M.M. (1969). *Toward a new curriculum in physical education*. New York: McGraw-Hill.

Magill, R.A. (1985). *Motor learning concepts and applications*. Dubuque, IO: Wm. C. Brown.

Magoon, R.A. (1973). *Education and psychology—past, present and future*. Columbus, Ohio: Charles E. Merrill Publishing Co.

Mahoney, E.R. (1979). "Sex education in the public schools: a discriminant analysis of characteristics of pro and anti individuals," *Journal of Sex Research*. 15:264-275.

Marland, S.P., Jr. (1971). "Environmental education cannot wait," *American Education*. 7:7.

Marsh, J.J. (1984). "Measuring affective objectives in physical education," *Physical Education*. 41:77-81.

Martin, B.L. & Briggs, L.J. (1986). *The Affective and Cognitive Domains: Integration for Instruction and Research*. Englewood Cliffs, NJ: Educational Technology Publications.

Massari, D.J. (1975). "The relation of reflection-impulsivity to field dependence-independence and internal-external control in children," *Journal of Genetic Psychology*. 126:61-67.

McGee, R. (1982). "Uses and abuses of affective measurement," *Journal of Physical Education, Recreation, and Dance*. 53:21-22.

McNab, W.L. (1981). "Advocating elementary sex education," *Health Education*. 12:22-25.

Messick, S. (1977). Individuality and Learning (Chapter 2). San Francisco: Jossey-Bass. Tomado de Garcia Ramos, J.M. (1982). "Hacia una valoracion del constructo dependencia-independencia de campo perceptivo," *Bordon*. 245:612.

Moskowitz, G. (1978). *Caring and sharing in the foreign language class*. Rowley, Mass.: Newbury House Publishers.

Montalvo, F.F. (1981a). *Mexican American culture simulator for child welfare: casework vignettes volume I and II*. San Antonio, TX: Worden School of Social Service, Our Lady of the Lake University of San Antonio.

————. (1981b). *Trainer's manual: Mexican American culture simulator for child welfare*. San Antonio, TX: Worden School of Social Service, Our Lady of the Lake University of San Antonio.

————. (1983). "Cross-Culture Social Work Education," *Journal of Social Work Education*. 19:48-53.

Montalvo, F.F., Lasater, T.T., & Gorza, N. (1981c). *Technical report: the Mexican American culture simulator for child welfare*. Mimeographed. San Antonio, TX: Worden School of Social Service, Our Lady of the Lake University of San Antonio.

Montalvo, F.F., Lasater, T.T., & Valdez, N.G. (1982). "Training child welfare workers for cultural awareness: the culture simulator technique," *Child Welfare League of America*. 61:341-352.

Mood, D. (1982). "Evaluation in the affective domain? No!" Journal of Physical Education, Recreation, and Dance. 53:18-20.

National Commission on Excellence in Education. (1983). *A nation at risk: the imperative for educational reform*. Washington, D.C.: U.S. Department of Education.

Nebes, R.D. (1975). "Man's so-called 'minor' hemisphere," *UCLA Educator*. 17:13-16.

New Jersey State Department of Education. (1981). *New Jersey family life guidelines. Trenton, N.J.: N. J. State Department of Education.*

Ninty-first Congress. (1970). Public law 91-516. Washington, D.C.: U. S. Government Printing Office.

Oxendine, J.B. (1984). *Psychology of motor learning*. Englewood Cliffs, N.J.: Prentice-Hall.

Packer, J. & Bain, J.D. (1978). "Cognitive style and teacher-student compatibility," *Journal of Educational Psychology*. 70:864-871.

Raths, L.E., Harmin, E.M., & Simon, S.B. (1966). *Values and teaching: working with values in the classroom*. Columbus, OH: Charles Merrill.

Rink, J. (1985). *Teaching physical education for learning*. St. Louis, MO: Time Mirror: Mosby College Publisher.

Romey, B. (1976). *Confluent Education in Science*. Canton, NY: Ash Lad Press.

Ryan, W. (1971). *Blaming the victim*. New York: Pantheon Books.

Sage, G.H. (1984). *Motor learning and Control*. Dubuque, IO: Wm. C. Brown.

Santos Rego, M.A., Doval Salgado, L., Sobrado Fernandez, L.M., & Sonnier, I.L. (1987). "A strategy for empirically evaluating holistic teaching," *Reading Improvement*. 23:277-287.

de los Santos, A., Montemayor, T., & Solis, E. (1981). "Chicano students in higher education: access, attrition and achievement," *La Red/The Net 41: Monthly Newsletter of the National Chicano Research Network*, University of Michigan.

Scales, P. (1982). "'Values' roles in sexuality education," *Planned Parenthood Review*. 2:6-8.

Shah, F. & Zelnik, M. (1981). "Parent and peer influence on sexual behavior, contraceptive use, and pregnancy experience of young women," *Journal of Marriage and the Family*. 43:339-348.

Shulman, L. (1979). *The skills of helping individuals and groups*. Itasca, IL: F.E. Peacock, Publisher.

Siedentop, D. (1980). *Physical education introductory analysis*. Dubuque, IO: Wm. C. Brown.

Simon, S.B. & Olds, S.W. (1977). *Helping your child learn right from wrong: A guide to values clarification*. New York: McGraw-Hill.

Simpson, E.J. (1966). "The classification of educational objectives: psychomotor domain," *Vocational and Technical Educational Grant Contract No. OE-85-104*. Washington, D.C.: Department of Health, Education, and Welfare.

Sonnier, I.L. (1975). "A model of contemporary philosophies used in a science teacher education program," *Science Education*. 59:221-227.

_____. (1976). "Logic patterns and individual differences," *The Southern Journal of Educational Research*. 10:136-150.

_____. (1981). "The open classroom: quantity and quality education," *Education*. 102:124-129.

_____. (1982a). "Debates evolving from cerebral hemisphere research," *Journal of College Science Teaching*. 12:4243.

_____. (1982b). *Holistic education: teaching of science in the affective domain*. New York: Philosophical Library Publishers.

_____. (1982c). "Holistic education: how I do it," *College Student Journal*. 16:64-69.

_____. (1982d). "Holistic education: teaching in the affective domain," *Education*. 103:11-14.

_____. (1984). "Debates updated: the educational implications of cerebral hemisphericity research," *Journal of College Science Teaching*. 13:376-378.

_____. (Ed.). (1985a). *Methods and techniques of holistic education*. Springfield, IL.: Charles C. Thomas, Publisher.

_____. (1985b). "The interfaces of human interactions in education," *College Student Journal*. 19:294-297.

Sonnier, I.L. & Kemp, J.B. (1980). "Teach the left brain and only the left brain learns, teach the right brain and both brains learn," *The Southern Journal of Educational Research*. 14:63-70.

Sonnier, I.L. & Wesselmann, D.M. (1984). "HOW and WHY to teach in the affective domain and become a more effective teacher," *Reading Improvement*. 21:220-226.

Sonnier, I.L. & Santos Rego, M.A. (1984). "Una revision de las implicaciones educativas de la investigacion sobre la hemispheridad cerebral (1)," *Quinesia: Revista de Educacion Especial*. (Marzo):23-26.

Sonnier, I.L. & Santos Rego, M.A. (1984). "Una revision de las implicaciones educativas de la investigacion sobre la hemispheridad cerebral (2)," *Quinesia: Revista de Educacion Especial*. (Decembro):5-10.

Sonnier, I.L. & Dow M.G. (1985). "The right hemisphere: seat of emotion colors," *Education*. 105:373-375.

Spirduso, W.W. (1978). "Hemispheric lateralization and orientation in compensatory and voluntary movement." In Stelmach, G.E. (Ed.). *Information processing in motor control and learning*. (pp. 289-309). New york: Academic Press.

Stefano Di, J.J. (1969), *Interpersonal perceptions of field-independent and field-dependent teachers and students*. Doctoral Dissertation, Cornell University.

Stelmach, G.E. (1978). *Information processing in motor control and learning*. New York: Academic Press.

Stoner, L.J. (1982). "Evaluation in the affective domain? Yes!" *Journal of Physical Education*. 53:16-17.

Templin, T.J. (1981). "Student as socializing agent," *Journal of Teaching Physical Education*, 1:71-79.

Toffler, A. (Ed.). (1974). *Learning for tomorrow: the role of the future in education*. New York: Random House.

Tomlinson, P. (1984). *Psicologia Educativa*. Madrid: Piramide.

Torrence, E.P., Reynolds, C.R., Riegel, T., & Ball, O. (1977). "Your learning and thinking, Form A and B: preliminary norms, abbreviated technical notes, scoring keys, and selected references," *The Gifted Child Quarterly*. 21:563-569.

Tousignant, M. & Siedentop, D. (1983). "A qualitative analysis of task structure in required secondary physical education classes. *Journal of Teaching Physical Education*. 3:47-57.

U.S. Department of Health and Human Services. (1985). "Summary of findings from national children and youth fitness study," *Journal of Physical Education, Recreation, and Dance*. 56:43-90.

U. S. Federal Register. (1980). "Nondiscrimination on the basis of race, creed and national origin under programs receiving federal financial assistance through the Department of Health and Human Services." September 17, 1980. p. 82972.

Vitale, B.M. (1982). *Unicorns are real: a right-brained approach to learning*. Rolling Hills Estate, CA 90274: Jalmar Press.

Watkins, R.K. (1926). Quoted in *A digest of investigations in teaching science*, by F. D. Curtis. Philadelphia, PA: P. Blakiston's Sons & Co., p. 99-100.

Wiese, C. (1982). "Is affective evaluation possible?" *Journal of Physical Education, Recreation, and Dance*. 53:23-24.

Williams, L.V. (1983). *Teaching for the two-sided mind: a guide to right brain/left brain education*. New York: Simon & Schuster, Inc.

Wilson, D. (1969). "Diversities of meanings of physical education," *Research Quarterly*. 40:211-214.

Witelson, S. (1977). "Developmental dyslexia: two right hemispheres and none left," *Science*. 195:309-311.

Witkin, H.A., Moore, C.A., Goodenough, D.R., & Cox, P.W. (1977). "Field dependent and field-independent cognitive styles and their educational implications," *Review of Educational Research*. 47:1-64.

Witkin, H.A. y Goodenough, D.R. (1985). *Estilos cognitivos: naturaleza y origenes*. Madrid: Piramide.

Witkin, S.L. (1979). "Cognitive processes and the intuitive practitioner: implications for practice," *Journal of Social Work*, in press. Presented at the National Association of Social Work Symposium, San Antonio, Texas.

Wittrock, M.C. (Ed.). (1986). *Handbook of research on teaching*. New York: Macmillan Publishing Company.

Zenhausern, R. (1982). "Education and the left hemisphere." In J.W. Keefe. (Ed.). *Student learning styles and brain behavior* (pp. 192-195). Reston, VA: National Association of Secondary School Principals.

INDEX